Corruption & Development Aid

Corruption & Development Aid

Confronting the Challenges

Georg Cremer

translated by
Elisabeth Schüth

Viva Books

New Delhi | Mumbai | Chennai | Kolkata | Bangalore | Hyderabad | Kochi | Guwahati

First Indian Edition 2010

VIVA BOOKS PRIVATE LIMITED

- 4737/23 Ansari Road, Daryaganj, New Delhi 110 002
  E-mail: vivadelhi@vivagroupindia.net, Tel. 42242200
- Plot No. 76, Service Industries, Shirvane, Sector 1, Nerul, Navi Mumbai 400 706
  E-mail: vivamumbai@vivagroupindia.net, Tel. 27721273, 27721274
- Jamals Fazal Chambers, 26 Greams Road, Chennai 600 006
  E-mail: vivachennai@vivagroupindia.net, Tel. 28290304, 28294241
- B-103, Jindal Towers, 21/1A/3 Darga Road, Kolkata 700 017
  E-mail: vivakolkata@vivagroupindia.net, Tel. 22836381, 22816713
- 7, Sovereign Park Apartments, 56-58, K. R. Road, Basavanagudi, Bangalore 560 004
  E-mail: vivabangalore@vivagroupindia.net, Tel. 26607409, 26607410
- 101-102 Mughal Marc Aptt., 3-4-637 to 641, Narayanguda, Hyderabad 500 029
  E-mail: vivahyderabad@vivagroupindia.net, Tel. 27564481, 27564482
- First Floor, Beevi Towers, SRM Road, Kaloor, Kochi 682 018, Kerala
  E-mail: vivakochi@vivagroupindia.net, Tel: 0484-2403055, 2403056
- 232, GNB Road, Beside UCO Bank, Silpukhuri, Guwahati 781 003
  E-mail: vivaguwahati@vivagroupindia.net, Tel: 0361-2666386

Published by arrangement with

Lynne Rienner Publishers Inc.
1800 30th Street, Boulder,
Colorado 80301
USA

ISBN 978-81-309-1225-7

Published by Vinod Vasishtha for Viva Books Private Limited, 4737/23, Ansari Road, New Delhi - 110 002. Printed and bound by Anand Sons, Delhi - 110 092.

for Hildegard

Contents

Foreword

CONCERN ABOUT THE EFFECTS OF CORRUPTION ON AID motivated a number of us in the early 1990s to start fighting corruption. In my work on development projects and later as a representative of the World Bank in Kenya, I had observed time and again how deals between companies from the industrialized world and high-ranking local officials led to utterly dysfunctional "white elephant" investments, undermining governance, destroying the environment, and worst of all, harming people and their chances for progress. But my partners in development and I had been much less aware of corrupt practices related to the projects for which we shared responsibility. Our growing recognition of the impact of corruption on development was one of our prime reasons for founding Transparency International in 1992.

Since then, a lot has changed. Development organizations work hard to contribute to the fight against corruption. There are many websites offering relevant strategies, regulations, controls, sanctions, codes, and commitments, and many books and articles have been written about corruption and development. About corruption and development *assistance,* however, dramatically less can be found. Suspicion and charges related to corruption are even more damaging for an aid system already under pressure than for suspects in the public and private sector. Publicity about corruption in aid is therefore avoided, or is rejected as inappropriate and overblown generalization. This is especially problematic because, in our experience, transparency and an informed and educated public are a necessary component of fighting corruption successfully. The taboo surrounding the subject of corruption in development aid has protected it for many decades; where this taboo lingers, fighting corruption becomes more difficult.

But there are ways out of this dilemma, and this book offers one of them. The book promotes transparency and understanding about the reasons behind and the detailed mechanisms of corruption related to development assistance. It facilitates communication among people directly involved in development work, in local and international organizations at all levels. In its German-language edition, it has proven a favorite in teaching and learning about corruption in development cooperation. More broadly, it contributes to open dialogue about the risks and realities of corruption, a dialogue so essential to fighting it successfully.

The author, Georg Cremer, positions corruption that affects development assistance within the broad context of the societal and economic causes of corruption in general, both globally and nationally. This approach precludes unrealistic expectations such as zero tolerance or the withdrawal of aid from countries where corruption occurs daily. But while Dr. Cremer is frank about the prevalence of corruption, he does not encourage us to accept a corrupt environment as an excuse to tolerate corruption. Instead, analyzing risks and describing concrete steps to avoid or reduce them, his book translates into the everyday practice of development aid the experiences of the global anticorruption movement, where we have learned that understanding more about corruption helps us to combat it, and to cope with it.

— Peter Eigen
Founder and Chairman of the Advisory Council,
Transparency International

Preface

I HAVE BEEN PREOCCUPIED WITH THE PHENOMENON OF CORruption in development work ever since I went to Indonesia in 1986 to work as a project leader under contract with a German organization. I was not prepared for what confronted me. The dangers of corruption within my own project or in my immediate surroundings had not once been addressed during the half year in which I was otherwise very thoroughly prepared for my deployment.

I left to work for an Indonesian research institute for education and employment and to support it in qualifying its work and carrying out studies that would help the Indonesian government in making political-economic decisions. When I started to understand the relationships between the institute and the officials in various ministries, it became evident that the research assignments we received had a certain "side effect": part of the international aid earmarked for research was, at the least possible level of risk, being turned into additional income for underpaid office holders. This, of course, irritated me. At least as irritating was the fact that the corruption-related reports I submitted to my dispatching organization were considered more a bother than anything else. Corruption was a taboo subject in project work, left off the record as a matter of course. The reaction of my dispatching organization was completely normal back in the mid-1980s.

Taboos are harmful. They prevent development aid organizations from learning from the diverse experiences of their staff and from better restricting corruption within their projects. The aim of this book is to contribute to breaking taboos. Another goal is to support those who work in the field of development aid in any capacity—in project work, in the headquarters of aid organizations, in many private initiatives—when they confront corruption, to a small or to a large degree. I hope that private donors also find an answer to the question of whether or under what circumstances their money actually reaches the needy.

* * *

I would like to mention several people to whom I owe thanks. I thank E. J. Sawong, my Indonesian counterpart who passed away in 1987. With extraordinary openness he helped me to comprehend the system of "deviating funds." I thank my former superiors at the international department of Caritas Germany, who encouraged me to concentrate on issues of corruption control, even though it is an unusual topic among aid organizations. I am grateful to the students who attended my lectures on corruption control at the University of Freiburg and at the Swiss Federal Institute of Technology in Zurich (ETH Zurich) for their many helpful questions. My thanks go out to all who read and provided their critical comments on the manuscript for this book: Michael Berger, University of Freiburg; Rolf Kappel, ETH Zurich; Johannes Müller, SJ, College of Philosophy, Munich; Jakob Rösel, University of Rostock; as well as Christel Jost, Christoph Klitsch-Ott, Franz-Josef Vollmer, and Christine Wegner-Schneider of Caritas Germany. I am grateful to Ilse Buschmann at the Arnold-Bergstraesser Institute in Freiburg, who put the manuscript to a tough test of comprehensibility. Special thanks go to Elisabeth Schüth for translating the revised German version. Finally, I thank my wife for her encouragement, critical questions, and support.

—G. C.

1

Corruption in Development Aid: From Taboo to Political Action

FOR A LONG TIME CORRUPTION HAS BEEN A TABOO SUBJECT among the institutions of development cooperation, in particular corruption occurring within their very own work. In line with the official viewpoint, development work oddly remains free of the effects of a problem that rages in most countries where aid is provided. Until the recent past, aid organizations seldom made an issue of bribery or embezzlement as a hindrance in carrying out the projects and programs they fund. Well-known evaluations of development aid have simply ignored this problem. The Cassen Report, published in 1986 and commissioned by the governments of eighteen donor countries, satisfies its readers with the following succinct statement: "This report does not discuss corruption. In some notorious countries, aid activities have added costs due to corruption by officials and others. But again, this is a phenomenon affecting only a small proportion of aid; much aid is disbursed only when the equipment or construction or technical cooperation it pays for is supplied or built, which considerably reduces the scope for illicit behavior."[1] As late as 1997, the German government argued similarly: "The misuse of aid funds through corrupt practice is *prevented* by strict protection and control mechanisms" (emphasis added). The government based its statement on "numerous protection and control mechanisms" it believes are working effectively, in particular avoiding payment in cash, requiring open bidding procedures, and implementing various controls in Germany and on site.[2]

The German Federal Ministry for Economic Cooperation and Development (BMZ) has propagated official optimism: "Numerous tight precautionary measures reduce to a minimal level the danger of corruption in allocating aid funds to foreign governments."[3] Though practices deemed corrupt have long occurred in development aid, they have, up until a short time ago, constituted a fringe phenomenon from an uncontested official point of view. In the worst case, such practices have resulted in added costs for aid projects.

A Problem That Should Not Exist

The official point of view is quite peculiar because development aid is allocated to governments and nongovernmental organizations (NGOs) in countries where everybody experiences corruption on a daily basis. Development projects are inevitably implemented under circumstances characterized by a lack of transparency and legal security. An assumption made by David Gould in an early paper on the problem of corruption in development aid still rings true today: If misuse and embezzlement are the order of the day in allocating the national budget, then there is no reason to believe that resources provided to the same offices from outside are not used in the same manner.[4]

In 2004 the US Senate Committee on Foreign Relations organized three hearings on combating corruption in the multilateral development banks. Richard Lugar, the chairman of the Senate Foreign Relations Committee, reported that an estimated rate of misuse of between 5 percent and 25 percent would mean that, of the $525 billion the World Bank has lent since 1946, between $26 billion and $130 billion had been misused.[5] Other multilateral and bilateral donors could also similarly calculate the impact of ignoring the problem of corruption in development aid for so many years.

Later in this book, I will explain in detail to what extent controls imposed from the outside can keep development work from succumbing to conditions of widespread corruption in recipient countries. Yet even if we were successful in shielding single aid projects from corruption, fears would still linger that recipient governments might use aid funds to finance other, already planned expenditures in order to free up funds they could then misappropriate without foreign controls.[6]

There is no disputing that corruption is widespread in developing countries, in the form of bribery as well as embezzlement. Due to a lack of other resources, large-scale investment in developing countries with low per capita income, and especially in the poorest of developing countries, is primarily financed by development aid.

Therefore, large-scale embezzlement in the public sector cannot be organized without involving foreign aid.

Furthermore, misused development aid has added to the debt burden of developing countries. As Manish Bapna stated in the hearing before the Senate Foreign Relations Committee mentioned above, multinational development banks (MDB) have unique institutional characteristics in that they are repaid by borrowing countries out of general revenues. "In the world of MDB lending there is no institutional financial risk in approving loans which in significant part are not used for the economic and social investments intended."[7]

The problem of corruption has been ignored by official aid organizations not only at the level of project implementation but also at a second level. For a long time, aid officials did not consider themselves responsible for improving the conditions for corruption control within developing countries. Up until the mid-1990s, the World Bank, the strongest financially and the leader in conceptual work among all official channels, believed it was not compatible with its mandate to become active in this field because it was impermissible to meddle in the domestic political affairs of recipient countries.[8] Well into the end of the 1990s, the country programs of the World Bank seldom directly addressed the problem of corruption, because, according to its own view, they had to take into account borrower sensitivity. In addition, there was uncertainty among World Bank staff on how to deal with corruption.[9] Bilateral governmental donors also kept an extremely low profile on this issue for a long time. They showed restraint because of the diplomatic considerations mentioned above, and therefore refused to deal seriously with corruption in their own projects. Donors' inattention to corruption was also bolstered by a wide range of political science and economic literature that supposedly documented a series of positive effects of corrupt practices, effects I will later examine more closely. Although this position is outdated according to current scientific literature, it is still alive in the institutions that sponsor development aid, due to the usual delay in the reception of scientific findings.

The Beginning of Political Change

The taboo is increasingly being broken, however. Corruption control in providing aid is becoming a political field of action. The World Bank had been intervening in the domestic politics of recipient countries for years, going back to its structural adjustment programs in the 1980s. "Crisis of governance" became the focus of World Bank analyses. Through its programs, the World Bank claimed to be improving governance and, with it, the conditions for economic and social development that are at the core of its mandate.[10] Despite its focus on *good governance*, however, the World Bank avoided speaking frankly about corruption in recipient countries. Not until Bank president James Wolfensohn took office in 1995 was a breakthrough achieved. In his speech to the World Bank annual assembly in 1996, Wolfensohn announced a turn toward openness in corruption control politics and did not hold back on making corruption a central topic within project work funded by the World Bank.

The significance of these changes has been compared to the decision by Robert McNamara in 1968 to elevate the fight against poverty to a central World Bank goal. There were doubts shortly after his speech as to whether Wolfensohn's policy transformation would survive his term in office.[11] In the decade that has passed since his speech, the World Bank has institutionalized its anticorruption policy[12] and taken a number of steps to implement it, such as establishing a Department of Institutional Integrity and a Sanctions Committee vested with the power to recommend bans on firms and individuals involved in fraudulent and corrupt practices from participation in further World Bank–financed projects, and, very recently, it began to disclose information regarding the results of its investigations in its annual integrity reports.[13] In March 2007 the World Bank board endorsed a strategy to scale up assistance to improve governance and fight corruption in recipient countries.[14] These and other steps provide hope for endurance.[15]

The policy change is based on more than Wolfensohn's personality. The most important prerequisite was the end of the Cold War. For governments funding development aid and their institutions, there was no longer an advantage to providing aid to corrupt governments in order to keep recipients loyal to their own political camp.[16] After the end of the Cold War, African nations in particular experienced a dramatic drop in significance, which weakened their ability to negotiate with donor governments. Under these circumstances it was much easier to limit the sovereignty of recipient countries by conditioning the means of development aid. A change in World Bank or bilateral donor policy similar to Wolfensohn's initiative back in the 1960s, 1970s, or the first part of the 1980s might well have resulted in politically awkward situations. Donor countries may have had to abstain from awarding extensive aid packages to notoriously corrupt recipient governments, even when doing so may have seemed opportune in fortifying political fronts in the confrontation between the Western and Eastern blocs.

Additional political developments have eased the process of breaking the taboo surrounding corruption in development aid: Democratization movements that followed the end of the Cold War enabled people in recipient countries to talk more openly about corruption in the state sector than in the past. It is far more difficult for donors to ignore a problem when it has become the focus of heated debate within recipient countries. Numerous developing economies have firmly integrated themselves into the world market; in the competition for investment, the reliability of state action has gained significance as a determinant of international competitiveness among recipient countries.[17] At the same time, in the scientific struggle with corruption phenomena, those who thought corruption in developing countries could increase efficiency lost ground; they had seen corruption as an instrument for limiting the great and thus damaging powers of the state.[18] Their analysis doubtless fostered the long-prevailing ignorance among development officials regarding corruption. Their ignorance was further challenged by the founding of Transparency International in the 1990s, now a globally active civil society organization that demands that governments create policies to control corruption. In addition, there are plenty of staff members within sponsoring organizations, including the World Bank, who are circumspect enough to notice that their work is being counteracted by epidemic corruption in recipient countries. They therefore push for greater attention to the issue of good governance in general and possibilities for corruption control in particular.

The World Bank proclamation and implementation of a change in policy does not necessarily mean that other multilateral donors and the bilateral donors follow suit. After all, it has been only a few years since the German government made the statement quoted at the beginning of this chapter, a statement that stems from the old spirit of ignorance in respect to corruption phenomena in development aid. A synthesis of lessons learned about donor practices in fighting corruption, prepared for the Development Assistance Committee (DAC) of the Organization for Economic Cooperation and Development (OECD) in 2003, stated that many donors still resist mainstreaming anticorruption measures for a variety of reasons, including lack of political leadership, the reluctance to adapt more confrontational approaches, the judgment that anticorruption is another fad that will fade away, and the fear that more openness on this issue would cause a public backlash against development aid.[19] The team preparing this synthesis report faced difficulties in collecting relevant documents from donors. In April 2003 the DAC secretariat requested donors to send examples of projects and activities that they felt reflected lessons learned in fighting corruption. Five donors (Australia, Canada, France, Switzerland, and the European Community) indicated that they did not feel they had adequate experience to contribute to the study.[20] Astonishingly, this statement was made by Switzerland, whose Head Office of Development and Cooperation submitted its concepts for corruption control, following a long internal discussion process, back in 1998.[21] In 2002, the German Federal Ministry for Economic Cooperation and Development published a paper on fighting corruption but largely omitted the issue of corruption in development projects; in 2008 it was still the official document.[22] Great Britain's Department for International Development (DFID) admits in its document, "Anti-corruption Strategy for DFID," that the World Bank took the lead in this field. According to DFID's assessment, "few development agencies have coherent anti-corruption strategies which they have actually implemented." DFID developed a broad approach in its anticorruption strategy, including combating bribery in international trade and deterring money laundering. On corruption in development aid, the DFID document is more specific than the German policy paper.[23] Norway has followed the World Bank's example and at least declared anticorruption as part of its strategies.[24] Other bilateral donors will eventually follow, with more or less hesitation, catalyzed by the World Bank's dominance in forming concepts for the field of development aid.

Because the World Bank has made an open issue of corruption, it is becoming increasingly difficult for other donors to claim that their own relationships to the recipients of their aid are not affected. In the future, donors will have to explain how they have integrated matters of corruption control into their own support policies. Development institutions kept silent for a long time, claiming in the internal debate that opening the issue of corruption would strengthen the position of those principally opposed to development work. In the future, opponents will gain the most ground whenever sponsoring organizations are not able to give a convincing answer to the question of how they deal with corruption. Even nongovernmental organizations (NGOs) will be held accountable, after years of premature praise when they did not have to prove that there is more transparency in their field than one usually encounters in the state sector.

The Plan of the Book

In the next chapter, I briefly define corruption and describe the most important areas of misuse of an office or a comparable position of trust for private purposes: bribery, misappropriation, and nepotism. In Chapter 3, I examine some of the common, and among development workers and experts some of the weightiest, arguments behind the supposed usefulness of corrupt practices in developing countries. Chapter 4 deals with various forms and degrees of corruption in development aid. Chapter 5 focuses on the consequences of corruption on performance in development projects and on decision processes on the part of recipient countries. Chapter 6 addresses the global aspects of corruption; here I argue that corruption is not a phenomenon to be explained in predominantly cultural terms. In Chapter 7, I show just how limited administrative control procedures are when there is no legal security and corruption is widespread in the government sector. Usually only the government sector is scrutinized for corruption; therefore, Chapter 8 takes a look at NGOs. Chapters 9 and 10 furnish proof that institutional impediments within development organizations of donor countries, such as barriers to information and disbursement pressure, often make it difficult and sometimes even impossible to effectively check corruption. Chapter 11 summarizes the results of the previous chapter in a "weakness checklist" that might be helpful in evaluating projects. Chapter 12 recommends steps in how to confront the challenges of controlling corruption in development aid and categorizes the subject within the broader framework of reform politics in developing countries.

Notes

1. Cassen et al. (1986), p. 13.
2. German Federal Government (1997).

3. BMZ press release 04-E 1001-34/97.
4. Gould (1979), pp. 261–262.
5. Lugar (2004), p. 1.
6. On the effects of freeing up funds in this manner, see Hemmer (1988), pp. 746–747, 790–791; Bastøe and Masst (2001), p. 73; and Wolff (2005), pp. 261ff.
7. Bapna (2004), p. 3.
8. See Johnson (1998), p. 2.
9. World Bank (1997a), p. 50.
10. Johnson (1998), p. 20; Caufield (1997), pp. 195–196. World Bank (1997a), pp. 23ff, provides the official viewpoint of the World Bank on the interpretation of its mandate regarding corruption control. In this viewpoint, the Bank shall limit itself to the economic aspects of corruption control but refrain from getting involved in political affairs. In reality, such a separation cannot be sustained.
11. Johnson (1998), pp. 20–21.
12. Aguilar, Gill, and Pino (2000); World Bank (2000, 2002a, 2005).
13. World Bank (2005); World Bank (2007a).
14. World Bank (2007b).
15. Paul Wolfowitz, who followed Wolfensohn as World Bank president in 2005, maintained the anticorruption policy of the Bank. He was forced to resign in 2007 due to his involvement in a decision to promote his companion, a Bank employee, before she was given an assignment at the US State Department because of their partnership. Wolfowitz's successor, Robert Zoellick, has maintained the anticorruption policy.
16. Johnson (1988), pp. 5–6.
17. Gray and Kaufmann (1998), p. 9.
18. See Chapter 3 in this volume.
19. Bailey (2003), p. 31.
20. Ibid., p. 15.
21. DEZA (1998). DEZA stands for the Direktion für Entwicklung und Zusammenarbeit/Head Office of Development and Cooperation.
22. BMZ (2002, 2007), p. 12, fn 9.
23. DFID (1999/2002). See also Anger (2004), pp. 35ff.
24. NORAD (2000). See also Anger (2004), pp. 32ff.

2

What Is Corruption?

CORRUPTION IS A WORD WITH A BROAD RANGE OF USES IN everyday speech. It is closely tied to both designating the facts and passing moral judgment and condemnation. *Corrupt* is used to describe a wide spectrum of behaviors in an individual's economic and political environment from illicit or illegitimate behavior to behavior that is simply considered undesirable by the person using the word. Accusing a political opponent of corruption is thus the ideal way to defame him or her.[1] As a scientific term, corruption is mainly used in the context of sociology and political science. Lacking the certainty of fact, it cannot be used as a legal term. In legalese, each offense is more narrowly defined: bribery, venality, acceptance of benefit, granting of benefit, and so on.[2] An enigmatic term with poor selectivity is also not suitable for analyzing development aid. It is thus now important to explain the meaning of corruption as it is used in this book.

Social scientists understand corruption as the misuse of an office or a comparable position of trust for private purposes. Given that definition, several prerequisites are set for using the term *corruption.*[3] At least one of the people involved in the behavior characterized as corrupt holds an office, but it need not be a public office: It is an area of responsibility defined by others. For example, a manager in a nongovernmental aid organization holds a position of trust that he or she could misuse for private purposes. There are standards, whether put forth by law or anchored in social consent, that determine how an office or a position of trust should be fulfilled. The behavior of those involved in a corrupt act is either illegal or at least contradictory to the behavioral norms associated with the office. The breach of office norms occurs consciously and intentionally to the advantage of the person holding the office. Gains can be material or immaterial and directly or indirectly beneficial to the person in office. Prestige attained by a corrupt act constitutes immaterial gains. Privileges for family members are an example of indirect gains achieved by the misuse of an official position.

The following three areas of misuse by officials should be included here in the definition of corruption: bribery, misappropriation of funds entrusted to an official, and nepotism. Here the term *corruption* is more narrowly defined than its corresponding usage in everyday speech or in political debate. These three areas suffice for an analysis of corruption in aid. They comprise clearly distinguishable facts and exclude the risks of a catchall concept.[4]

Bribery

Bribery is a trade-off between two participants or two groups of participants, one who bribes and one who accepts a bribe.[5] The one who bribes receives, in exchange for money (the bribe) or some kind of good, a service that he would otherwise not have received at all, or not with certainty, or not until a later point in time. The corrupt service might be the issuance of a license or the awarding of a public contract to the one who does the bribing. The one who accepts a bribe is an official or holds a similar position of trust. In guaranteeing a bribed service and in accepting a bribe, an official misuses his position and thus breaches the norms tied to his position.

The one who bribes is commonly referred to as the "active" participant, whereas the one who accepts a bribe is referred to as the "passive" participant. This choice of words is unfortunate because the "passive" participant can very actively offer corrupt services and demand bribe payments. The "passive" one can also improperly exploit the scope of power inherent in his position in order to limit the options of the "active" participant to such a degree that he cannot pursue his own legitimate interests without consenting to a bribe contract.

To better understand bribery, it would be helpful to categorize services traded for money or for gains with a monetary value into several groups.[6] The following classification is also useful in analyzing bribery within the context of development aid:

1. In a bribery contract, selection procedures can be influenced to favor the briber. The briber secures his receipt of a certain good that he would otherwise not receive at all, or not with certainty. He receives—in rationing, for example—greater amounts of the desired item or can evade exclusion regulations.

2. In an existing contractual relationship, the one offering the bribe secures higher profits for himself by, for example, seeing to it that the person he bribes changes the price, the supplier conditions, or the quality requirements in a public contract.

3. The briber expedites decision processes and/or general administrative processes. In doing so, he wards off costs otherwise incurred by delays.

4. The bribe serves to secure an illegal deal that has already been committed or is being planned by paying off prosecuting authorities or law enforcement officials.

5. The briber wards off threats, obstacles, and difficulties arbitrarily imposed upon him by officials.

The last case alludes to the fact that a bribe is not always necessarily a voluntary act in a trade-off deal. There is a gray area between bribery and extortion, in which an official can arbitrarily impose negative consequences on his contractual partner if he refuses to pay a bribe. Extortion occurs when (1) people do not receive services they are legally entitled to without paying first; (2) an official abuses his discretionary powers to apply pressure on others to pay bribe money; or (3) false criminal accusations are made with the intention of forcing payment in exchange for dropping charges. The greater the degree of coercion attached to the payment an officer receives, the more dubious it is to assume there has been a trade-off between equal contractual parties and the more appropriate it is to define the deal not as a bribe by the payer to the official involved, but as extortion of the payer by the official.

Misappropriation

Officers misappropriate when they, in a deviant manner, acquire funds entrusted to them within the framework of their official duties. Misappropriation of public funds is effected by civil servants who have some scope in deciding how to allocate the state budget.

Misappropriation can occur by the individual deed of an official; as opposed to bribery, this offense does not require a contract with a partner. However, misappropriation is frequently more than just a question of deviant individual behavior on the part of lone officials.

Generally, groups of officials work together in misappropriating funds. Only by doing so is it possible for them to bypass inspections. Such rudimentary inspection mechanisms are even found in the administrations of countries where corruption is an everyday phenomenon. If that weren't the case, it would be impossible to maintain any public functions at all. The crudest cash register theft is forbidden as long as there is an administration around. In order to shut out control mechanisms and decrease the risk for officials involved, certain procedures have to be adhered to that make it difficult or even impossible to prove after the fact that misappropriation has occurred. To ensure no proof can be found, misappropriation is usually tied to falsifying receipts.[7] Knowledge of the procedures used to falsify receipts is essential for anyone who works in development aid, either in an operational or managerial position. The first part of Chapter 7 describes these procedures in detail. The most important procedure by far in securing misappropriation is the kickback tied to contracts awarded by corrupt officials. The party who wins the contract, in agreement with the official involved, charges more than the market price or the price that would have been set in a proper bidding procedure. The contractor then passes the extra charge, either entirely or in part, back to the official who awarded the contract. That official then keeps the amount paid back to him for private use. In the field of development aid, collusion in the procurement process, complemented by kickback and bribery, is very probably the most significant form of corruption in terms of frequency.[8]

The kickback has, for the official who receives it, an invaluable advantage in that the problem of reporting the misappropriated amount is shifted to the contractor. The kickback cannot be traced in the official's financial report because the money disbursed corresponds to the—excessive—total amount on the invoice. In a modified form of kickback, the price charged corresponds to the fair market price or to the price set in a proper bidding procedure. Nonetheless, money flows back to the official who awarded the contract, money obtained when the contractor provides lower quality goods or cuts back on services agreed upon in the contract. The consequences of kickback agreements for the selection and implementation of aid projects are discussed separately in Chapter 5.

Large-scale misappropriation cannot occur at the hands of an individual official, as a rule, if for no other reason than because several officials have to participate in financially extensive programs and because administrative control mechanisms have to be bypassed. Thus, it is essential to form a group to carry out successful misappropriation schemes.

Profits from misappropriation have to be shared among those who participated in decisionmaking, as well as with those who are aware of relevant insider information. Internal supervisory committees or external planning and supervisory authorities may have to be included in the distribution mechanism of misappropriated funds. When such authorities demand payment from subordinate offices in exchange for the approval of a project or the certification of its proper implementation, they secure a portion of the extralegal income for themselves. And they assume—rightly so, in an environment of epidemic corruption—that said income would be made even without their intervention. If a misappropriation ring is revealed, ring members also have to cover themselves by paying off criminal prosecution authorities. In order to manage such a bulky distribution mechanism, it is sometimes necessary for the officials involved to run an informal pool, especially when payments for project approval or payments to inspectors and income from misappropriation do not fall into the same time frame.[9]

Misappropriation schemes and, in particular, kickback agreements are often linked to bribery. When some of the misappropriated funds are passed on to control authorities, a bribe has occurred, whereby the bribery actually serves to ensure the illegal act of misappropriation.

Bribery can coincide with a kickback agreement when the officer in charge of awarding a contract is paid off so that selection within the procurement process occurs in favor of the kickback partner. Or the kickback partner can raise the returns of his contract with an official institution by agreeing to pay just a part of the amount over market value back to officials. Bribery and misappropriation can therefore be very closely linked and—especially within the context of development aid—drawn together as one component of the corruption phenomenon.[10]

Nepotism

We speak of nepotism when an official position is exploited to give preference to individuals or groups with whom the officer has a close relationship. In particular, nepotism occurs when an official abuses his position to control access to employment in an official circle. The official responsible for recruitment favors, in disregard of existing rules, members of his family, his own ethnic group, people from his home region, or people with the same political leaning. In a broader sense, we speak of nepotism when an official gives preferential treatment to said people in awarding privileges, such as licenses or contracts. Looking back to the beginning of this chapter at the basic definition of corruption as the abuse of an office for private purposes, we may ask what private interests are met by an official committing nepotism. There might be an immaterial advantage, for example, the simple satisfaction of fulfilling traditional obligations of solidarity in regard to family or other social groups.[11]

An officer's personal interests may, however, go beyond that. In recruiting on the basis of nepotism, an official active in corrupt schemes elsewhere can secure his position. Since corruption does not usually occur at the hands of an individual acting alone, an official cannot do without accessories within his administration. A corrupt official can more easily make secret arrangements and check adherence to them with people who are indebted to him for their jobs and are also related to him or share his ethnic or regional background than with people with whom he does not have such a relationship.[12] A direct material advantage can be linked most closely to the official who commits family nepotism. In doing so, he secures his own social status because he will most likely receive reciprocal favors. A family member who has stepped into a position through nepotism might climb the career ladder and later show his appreciation to the relative who initially helped him or to the children of that relative.

Notes

1. Fleck and Kuzmics (1985), pp. 7ff.
2. See Kaiser (1991), p. 28. *Corruption,* as seen in the US Foreign Corruption Practices Act, is used as a synonym for bribery.
3. See, in particular, Neugebauer (1978), pp. 5ff (regarding bribery); Heidenheimer, Johnston, and Le Vine (1999), pp. 8ff; Pritzl (1997), pp. 47ff. In this book, I follow a rules-oriented definition of corruption that, according to Pritzl (1997), p. 55, and Kurer (2003), p. 45, is most widely used.
4. The narrow definition here follows Nye (1967/1999), p. 966.
5. This presentation follows Neugebauer (1978), pp. 6–13. Compare also Borner and Schwyzer (1999), pp. 21ff.

6. See Neugebauer (1978), pp. 11ff, and Pritzl's expansion on it (1997), pp. 94ff.

7. See Van Klaveren (1957), pp. 318–319. Van Klaveren refers to time prior to the French Revolution. Some of the types of "receipt production" he describes sound very current.

8. From the 441 allegations on fraud and corruption in Bank-financed projects that the World Bank closed in fiscal years 2005 and 2006, 36 percent were about collusion in the procurement process and 38 percent about kick-backs and bribes, often a component of collusion during the bidding process. See World Bank (2007a), pp. 8–9.

9. Cremer (1990), pp. 217–218.

10. Some literature on economics uses *corruption* as a synonym for *bribery*. See, for example, Neugebauer (1978), pp. 5–6. I do not subscribe to this narrow usage of the term *corruption.*

11. Pritzl (1997), p. 115.

12. On the implementation of corrupt contracts, see the very interesting analysis by Lambsdorff (1997, 1999b, 2002); and Lambsdorff and Teksoz (2005).

3

How Useful Is Corruption?

THERE SHOULD BE NO DISPUTING THAT CORRUPTION HAS brought about negative consequences in Western societies. When evidence of corruption phenomena is found, nobody in Western societies considers the potential societal advantages of such corrupt occurrences. That is not the case when referring to developing countries, however. Some social science literature considers what Westerners would refer to as corrupt conduct as essential to keeping developing countries functioning.[1] This viewpoint has been strongly supported by economic literature. It has, however, always been disputed. Gunnar Myrdal vehemently opposed it early on in his book *Asian Drama.*[2] More recent works have shown that the claim that corruption has positive effects on development goals has lost substantial ground.[3] However, that very claim lives on in the organizations that sponsor development aid. Some of the arguments put forward cannot be easily dismissed. It is worthwhile to take a close look at them and, at the same time, at some of the effects of corruption on development.

Critics say that analysis of the effects of corruption should not be based on the fictitious ideal of an efficient, development-oriented bureaucracy. Rather, it should be aligned with the realities of a body of civil servants watching out for their own interests. If analysts concede that the bureaucracy in question pursues its own interests, interests that often do not overlap with the goals of economic and social development, then corruption can have positive effects in regard to the fulfillment of development goals. As Nathaniel H. Leff argued in his very influential essay, "Economic Development Through Bureaucratic Corruption," a negative evaluation of corruption is a prejudice held by those who consider governmental administrative activities the impetus to economic development.[4]

A Catalyst for Competition?

Bribery allows for the weakening or removal of development-unfriendly bureaucratic intrusions in the economic process. Further, it makes competition possible in situations in which the government restricts or abolishes competition. In fact, there are a number of development-unfriendly bureaucratic intrusions into the economic process that can be diminished or removed through bribery. In many countries, domestic industrial production is shielded from international competitors by customs duties and by a jungle of nontariff trade barriers. Corruption in customs administrations allows for the circumvention of trade limitations, thus sustaining a certain amount of competitive pressure for the domestic industry. Or a government intends to restrict or abolish domestic competition by issuing production licenses; the bribery mechanism enables those companies that produce most efficiently and dispose of the largest bribery potential to obtain licenses.[5] Or agricultural businesses are forced to sell their products to governmental monopoly organizations at below-market prices. Illegal markets, secured by bribing controllers, are of central importance to food supplies because they provide production incentives for agricultural businesses.

All of the above are examples of second-best solutions. Bribery mechanisms cannot completely remove the negative effects of governmental intervention, but the effects are supposedly better than if all people strictly obeyed the law. This observation lies at the core of the debate over the potential advantages of corruption. Samuel P. Huntington emphasizes its importance: "In terms of economic growth, the only thing worse than a society with a rigid, overcentralized, dishonest bureaucracy, is one with a rigid, overcentralized, honest bureaucracy."[6]

However, before we interpret bribery primarily as a mechanism for circumventing development-unfriendly bureaucratic intrusions, we should consider its far-reaching interrelations. Where bribery is a widespread phenomenon, groups of civil servants follow strategies for maintaining and expanding their chances of being bribed. It is those interventions that can be circumvented that provide chances of being bribed. A bureaucracy whose officials profit substantially from bribes strongly resists reductions in state regulations. Such regulations could possibly be eliminated in a legal manner, but because of the connection between state-imposed hurdles and illicit additional income, there is a strong interest in upholding them. Thus the numerous, crude administrative rules found in developing countries not only serve as the basis for many bribe contracts but also result from a system of gaining illegal income for civil servants. Moreover, bribery is used not only as an instrument for warding off unfriendly state interference but also for achieving interference whenever it benefits bribers, such as in the creation, preservation, or expansion of restrictions on competition.[7]

Aligning state intervention with the briber's own interests is not the only object of bribery contracts. Another victim can be found in the governmental activities necessary for guaranteeing the legal framework for the actions of individuals and groups, including the framework for competition. Each and every contract is of debatable value when a contractual partner can evade adherence to the civil law governing contracts by bribing the judge, and when it is uncertain whether the partner who has acted according to the law has the means to compel the court to enforce justice. It is in the interests of bribers to ensure that the courts remain weak. The predictability of business dealings is thus restricted substantially by the conditions of a corrupt administration and a corrupt legal system.

There is a further objection to the claim that corruption promotes competitive processes under conditions of excessive governmental regulation. The argument in this case makes an analogy between the mechanism for bribery and a legal pricing system. Economic models that depict a mechanism for bribery (for example, the corrupt issuance of state licenses) assume that licenses are awarded by officials to the highest bidder.[8] In the end, the few licenses available go to those who can produce most efficiently and thus dispose of the greatest bribe potential. According to this model, everyone who is interested in obtaining the license offers a bribe to the corrupt public official, and the highest bidder wins, just as in a legal auction. Naturally, this scheme requires a free flow of information. The public official contacts many or potentially even all of the bidders and looks into their bribe offers. However, this assumption contradicts the fact that passive bribery is illegal and burdens public officials with risks they want to minimize. Corrupt officials prefer repetitive corruption contracts. If they award contracts or issue licenses on a regular basis, they prefer to reward those with whom they have already successfully and confidentially cooperated. They thus avoid the risk of being caught that is linked to every search for new partners. Moreover, with repetitive corruption contracts they can be sure of adherence to agreements that are neither fixed in writing nor subject to legal recourse.

The partners in a corruption contract make themselves dependent on each other, and they remain in this relationship of mutual dependency even after they have exchanged the agreed-upon service, for instance, a license and bribe money.[9] One partner could later report the other or blackmail him or her with the threat of doing so for whatever reason, should an opportune moment arise.[10] The corruption contract implies a vow of secrecy. The risk of that vow being broken is lower for public officials if they consistently seal corruption contracts with one or just a few partners. The risk calculations of corrupt officials thus create nearly insurmountable obstacles for newcomers who would like to enter the market, which clearly contradicts the viewpoint that bribery encourages competitive processes.

A further contradiction to that viewpoint is the fact that, in issuing licenses or other state privileges, officials who are aware of their risks would be wise to give preference to politically influential suppliers such as businesspeople close to the governing party or members of influential political families. Such people dispose of greater potential for defending themselves and can thus guarantee corrupt officials protection in case they are later prosecuted for their participation in corrupt activities. Of course, even a public bureaucracy considered incorruptible would feel pressure to favor politically influential suppliers. However, the risks arising from the illegality of bribed allocation produce that pressure just as well. And thus there is no substance to the claim that, in comparison to a legal allocation system in which politically influential suppliers are given priority, a system based on bribes regulates allocation primarily under the aspect of efficiency.

Less Red Tape?

Bribery, according to the arguments brought forth both by practitioners and in the scientific literature, speeds up bureaucratic processes.[11] It takes time to process information and to make decisions according to bureaucratic procedures; waiting periods often incur substantial costs for people who are dependent on a state license or other state services. Thus there are incentives for accelerating bureaucratic procedures through illegal payments. Applicants who face increased substantial costs with each day they wait will pay bribes in order to get priority service. In line with the argument mentioned above, waiting costs are minimized as a result, and inefficiency in public administrations is reduced. But we should take a look here at how bureaucratic behavior changes when it is possible to obtain bribed income. The hesitant manner of working found in many bureaucracies in developing countries largely results from strategic intention: Public officials can threaten those who depend on their services with delays that will incur costs, thus, in the end, forcing everyone to pay bribe money for services they have a legal right to receive.[12] Officials struggle over how to distribute chances for obtaining bribes and, with that, illegal income inside the bureaucracy; this struggle leads to a division of administrative responsibility and multiplied power of delay. As a result, victims face dwindling prospects of ever attaching the cause of bureaucratic delay to individual officials or official bodies. Victims also have fewer alternative ways of defending their rights other than paying "grease money." Recent empirical studies have asked more than 8,000 business leaders how common irregular payments are in their area of business and how much time they spend negotiating with officials over the interpretation of guidelines. In those places where grease money is often paid, managers spend particularly large amounts of time dealing with bureaucracy. A high level of bribery is coupled with high bureaucratic hurdles.[13]

Incentives for Qualified Civil Servants?

A further aspect should be considered in the evaluation of corruption in developing countries: How does corruption affect the level of qualification among officials in civil service? Is it not true that income from bribery and misappropriation under the prevailing circumstances provides irresistible motivation for qualified people to seek jobs in the civil service field? In many developing countries, the legal wages and privileges obtained by public service fall far short of what people with outstanding qualifications can earn in the private sector.[14] Therefore, legal salaries are not commensurate with qualification requirements. A raise in civil servant salaries across the board would fail on fiscal grounds, all the more since civil service has been expanded in many countries to absorb secondary school and university graduates into the employment system. The fact that the civil service sector remains highly attractive can be attributed to its high standing in society, to the high level of job security, and to the promise of protection in retirement years.[15] However, these aspects alone would not suffice to prevent a shift of qualified personnel from the public service into the private sector wherever there are crass differences in salaries. Under Suharto's reign in Indonesia, the rule of thumb was for public officials to spend three to four times their official salary in order to lead a lifestyle befitting their rank.[16]

Additional sources of income are necessary to compensate for salary differences between the public and the private sectors. Such sources can be found in bonuses or special privileges for managing projects or for business trip expenses. They lie within the realm of legal salary supplements. Such sources can also be found in the tacit tolerance of side jobs, moonlighting activities that are pursued by public officials at the expense of their regular working hours as long as official on-the-job attendance does not create any great obstacle. And compensation can be found in income from bribery and misappropriation. Income from corruption can be used to raise the total income of qualified staff members in a differentiated manner without raising salary levels in general. Public office managers are in a position to control who is placed in positions in which large amounts of corruption income can be obtained.

Whether individual qualification plays any role whatsoever in this placement process is another issue. At any rate, to simply view corruption as an alternative form of payment for civil servants is to underestimate the costs attached. First of all, there are the costs incurred by dirigiste intervention and the delays created to increase and distribute opportunities for bribery. Second, collectively organized misappropriation incurs costs far greater than the additional income made possible by it because bureaucratic decisions are influenced by minimizing risk. No bureaucracy can do without rudimentary mechanisms of financial control. Civil servants who embezzle funds prefer the types of budgetary expenditure items that can easily be tied to low-risk procedures of misappropriation. One such low-risk procedure is the extraction of kickback payments in investment projects. Often the very same people and official bodies responsible for cost-benefit analyses of investment projects also profit from the kickback payments to be had during project implementation. The Third World debt crisis, essentially caused by loan-financed public investment projects that could not make the profit needed to keep up with loan repayment schedules, cannot be adequately elucidated without taking the above kickback aspect into consideration.[17] I return to this subject in greater detail in Chapter 5, when I look at the consequences of corruption in development projects.

Illicit Income as an Essential Source of Capital Accumulation?

The effects corruption has on development depend, of course, on how income from corruption is spent. It could possibly be an essential source of capital accumulation. However, this argument makes sense only when we assume that the sum of income earned from corruption is not negligible in comparison with the national income, that corruption constitutes more than just a fringe phenomenon. Such an assumption should hold true for the majority of developing countries. Let us also assume that those who draw on income from corruption obtain a higher level of total income than those who make corruption payments. There are important corruption-based relationships in which this does not apply, for example, when businesspeople from the private sector bribe civil servants at the lower and middle levels of public service. Even if we assume that corruption leads to an economically relevant transfer of income to high-end earners, it does not necessarily lead to an increase in the rate of saving because consumption for prestige reigns among the political class of many developing countries. But even if the winners in the corruption game were to save more than the losers, it remains questionable whether they invest their income from corruption in the domestic economy. Schmidt expresses the following, rather scholastic notion: "In the interest of economic growth in the developing countries it would be desirable to see savings from corruption income invested domestically. A minimum amount of political and economic stability seems to be the indispensable requirement for achieving this goal."[18] However, contrary to this notion there is a strong tendency for income from corruption to be safely transferred to offshore destinations. Those in public administrative positions who gain high levels of income from corruption and thus possess large savings potential are, at the same time, dependent on fragile political loyalties. Any domestic investments they make are in danger of being expropriated as soon as those who have guaranteed political protection are no longer in power. If attempts are made at effective corruption control, the assets of a public official that are incompatible with his or her legal income become the target of suspicion for controlling authorities.[19] Domestic investments are much easier for controlling authorities to trace than assets that have been transferred abroad. If a policy of corruption control exists, the search for and confiscation of income from corruption will be an integral part of that policy. A serious control policy cannot grant legal immunity for investments financed by corruption income. Even if controls are lax at the time investment decisions are made, those who want to invest income from corruption can never be sure whether future governments might introduce serious controls and actually run legitimacy checks on assets. But even in certain political constellations in which those who profit from corruption have no need to fear any future intensification of controls, they may still prefer to invest abroad. As domestic investors they are confronted with all the obstacles created by bureaucracies to maintain and expand opportunities for bribery. Like all other investors in the country, they have to worry about whether they, at the time they decide to invest, can predict the amount of illegal payments required at a later point.[20] They have to determine whether the legal surroundings are stable enough to support their investment, even as the bribery they encourage erodes the legal framework. And when they make a domestic investment, they must depend on a publicly run infrastructure that will not perform well under conditions of widespread corruption in the government sector.

Bribery as a Means of Protecting Minorities?

A further argument claims that minorities can pay bribes to protect themselves from discrimination or, at least, to lessen the effects of discrimination. This argument should be taken seriously, particularly in societies with strong ethnic segmentation. Of course, only those minority groups who have the financial standing to afford bribe payments are able to protect themselves against discrimination. The financially successful Chinese minority in several countries of

Southeast Asia provides an example here. This type of protection is double-edged. The majority population considers any minority group that protects itself from discrimination by paying bribes as a collaborator with the corrupt political class. That compounds prejudices that already exist against financially successful minority groups. Stubborn prejudice makes discrimination easier and places hurdles in the way of integration for minorities.

A Balanced Assessment of Corruption

No single argument postulating the positive effects of corruption in developing countries is convincing enough to support the tacit tolerance of corruption in development aid. Recent multiple-country studies document the consequences of corruption on economic development. In these studies corruption is measured by various perception indexes based on surveys of consultants, experts, and firm managers. Corruption is negatively associated with domestic investment, reduces foreign investment, and affects domestic growth.[21] Certainly, there is space to argue that a single corrupt act, with all its effects and side effects, might do no harm or might even have a positive affect on development. But there is no way to limit corruption just to those acts that do no harm. On balance, multiple-country studies give overwhelming statistical evidence that countries with high corruption levels have poorer economic performance. They are more likely to have inadequate government supervision of the financial system and, therefore, are more likely to have vulnerable banks. Corruption influences the composition of public expenditure at the expense of health and education funds because these expenditures, compared to other public expenditures, are more difficult to misappropriate.[22] Corruption exacerbates destruction of the natural environment when environmental safeguards are often overcome with the help of bribes and when selection of projects depends on their ability to offer better opportunities for kickbacks and bribes.[23] And, to say the least, corrupt countries are less effective in supporting the poor.[24]

There is one argument from those claiming corruption may have positive effects under certain circumstances that may be taken seriously: bribery of controlling bodies can lessen the negative consequences of state intervention under conditions of rigid, dirigiste administration. In such cases, corruption as a remedy often lessens the power of obstacles set up or maintained by an administration with the purpose of obtaining corrupt income. Another aspect that must be taken seriously is the potential protection purchased through bribery by politically unpopular groups or persecuted ethnic groups. Without a bribable civil service apparatus, it would be easier to consistently oppress those groups. Corruption in development cooperation means, however, misappropriation by public officials as well as bribe contracts that secure misappropriation schemes. Donors who wish to use aid funds to increase civil service wages should do so by officially arranging for budget assistance in connection with talks concerning the reform of public service. The view that extensive embezzlement by civil servants can have positive effects on the attainment of aid goals cannot be supported seriously. The long-maintained neglect of corruption control issues by sponsoring organizations cannot, at any rate, be justified by potential advantages of corruption or by the supposedly ambiguous results of the analyses of the effects of corruption.

Notes

1. Discussion on this point is documented in detail in Heidenheimer, Johnston, and Le Vine (1999), especially pp. 375ff.
2. Myrdal (1968), pp. 937–958.
3. See, for example, Alam (1989, 1990); Bardhan (1997); Kaufmann and Wei (1999).
4. Leff (1964/1999), pp. 390–391.
5. Ibid., p. 396; a detailed formulation of this argument can be found in Neugebauer (1978), pp. 72ff.
6. Huntington (1968/1999), p. 386.
7. On the distortion of competition through corrupt acts, see Goudie and Stasavage (1997), pp. 39–40. See also Kaufmann (1997a).
8. See, for example, Neugebauer (1978), pp. 72ff.
9. See the analysis of this postenforcement lock-in from an institutional economics point of view in Lambsdorff (1999b), pp. 76ff; Lambsdorff and Teksoz (2005).
10. For example, when one is asked to serve as a principal witness or when the expected punishment is handed down one-sidedly. Lambsdorff (1997), pp. 13ff.
11. See Lui (1985). For critique see Bardhan (1997), p. 1323; Kaufmann and Wei (1999).
12. Myrdal (1968), pp. 952–953, made this point in referring to the results of an Indian inspection committee.
13. See Kaufmann and Wei (1999), pp. 6–13. Three surveys were done

for the Global Competitiveness Reports of 1996 and 1997, as well as for the World Development Report of 1997. Managers in Ukraine spend 30 to 40 percent of their working hours on dealings with civil servants. See Kaufmann (1997b), p. 7.

14. The World Bank (1997b), p. 9, states that, among developing countries in general, public officials at higher levels are underpaid. Sarah Bales and Martin Rama (2002) confirm this pattern in their study on Vietnam. Jobs found in formal sector enterprises are the relevant alternative for civil servants at the professional and managerial level. At that level underpayment is common. At lower ranks, self-employment or casual work in informal activities might be the relevant alternative. Based on this comparison, public sector workers might be overpaid. On salary levels in Indonesia, see RDCMD (1988), p. 44; Cremer (1995), pp. 213–214. A comparison, differentiated according to qualification levels, between the legal salaries of state employees and employees in private businesses in Indonesia shows that the level of earnings in the state sector falls below that of the private sector on all qualification levels, and that the discrepancy is noticeably greater at higher qualification levels than at lower levels.

15. On the privileges of state employees within the systems of social security in developing countries, see Articus (1990), pp. 158–160, 185ff. On recent policies to expand the coverage of social security systems, see van Ginneken (2003).

16. Hadisumarto (1974), p. 243; MacAndrews (1986), pp. 32–33. See also Gray (1979).

17. On the link between corruption and debt in one-party nations in Africa, see Tetzlaff (1991), pp. 51–54.

18. Schmidt (2003), p. 96. See also Schmidt and Garschagen (1978), p. 572.

19. See Klitgaard (1988), especially examples from Hong Kong and Singapore.

20. See Goudie and Stasavage (1997), pp. 37–38; World Bank (1997a), p. 69; Lambsdorff (2001), pp. 28–29. When making a political assessment of the effects of corruption on the type and size of investments in developing countries, one should also consider that, due to their weak defense position, small businesses may be hindered in their growth or even pushed into the informal sector. See de Soto (1992) on Peru.

21. Wei (1999), pp. 8ff.

22. Wei (2001); Tanzi and Davoodi (1997).

23. Eigen (2004), pp. 9–10.

24. See Kaufmann, Kraay, and Zoido-Lobatón (1999), pp. 17–18. The authors work with a set of six perception-based governance indicators, including the perception of corruption. Their analysis covering 150 countries shows a strong relationship between governance and development outcomes for all six indicators. Improved governance has a strong negative impact on infant mortality and leads to significant increases in adult literacy. On the uses and limitations of perception-based measures of governance, see Kaufmann, Kraay, and Mastruzzi (2003), pp. 19ff.

4

Corruption in Development Projects

CORRUPTION IS AN EVERYDAY PHENOMENON IN MANY countries where aid projects run.[1] Individuals responsible for implementing aid projects under such conditions constantly confront situations that compel them to enter into corrupt contracts in order to achieve progress. Such is the case when required state approval cannot be attained without "expediting payments" or when urgently needed goods cannot be imported without bribing customs officials. Strictly legal working methods might result in extremely negative consequences for reaching the goals of a project. Project leaders enter corrupt contracts under such conditions. They pay, for example, "expedition money" for a public service they actually have a legal right to. They do not make such payments in order to gain personal advantage, but rather to keep their projects free from risks caused by external factors. People in charge of projects are in the same situation as private investors confronted with a state bureaucracy that uses its decisionmaking powers to create opportunities for bribery. When a nation is in ruins, the remaining civil servants no longer receive regular wages and thus secure their own income by extorting illicit payments. Under these circumstances it is nearly impossible for project leaders to carry out projects without a willingness to make extralegal payments.[2]

Project leaders have to weigh whether and to what extent they are willing to enter corrupt contracts in order to move their projects along. The larger a project or the greater the accumulated bargaining leverage for aid sponsors who have supported several projects, the greater their responsibility for the conditions surrounding their work.

If sponsors cannot push through a sufficient number of requirements by threatening to cut off all further cooperation if corruption comes into play, or if it is impossible to create enough pressure in a combined effort by several aid organizations working in one area, then project leaders may become stuck in a *pay it or leave it* situation. Whenever project leaders enter into corrupt contracts with the sole aim of overcoming external obstacles to the implementation of their projects, then corruption is described as an external problem in project implementation. That subject will not be further discussed in this chapter. In this chapter I deal exclusively with corruption as an internal problem of development aid, in other words, when staff of aid organizations, decisionmakers, and anyone involved in carrying out a project misuses his or her position to gain extralegal advantages.

How Limited Is Empirical Access?

The illegality of corruption contracts and their resulting clandestine nature make it difficult to find empirical evidence of corruption. The actors in corrupt agreements are, naturally, not automatically willing to give interviews to researchers, in particular when they fear they might produce evidence against themselves in a prosecution. Case studies are based on confidential statements that might be challenged by those involved and that often cannot be confirmed or denied by third parties. The limitations of empirical studies long served as an argument against dealing closely with the issue of how much aid funding actually forms the basis for additional corrupt side income for civil servants in recipient countries. Whoever dared speak about this topic was quickly accused of unjustly generalizing individual cases. At the same time, the lack of an empirical foundation was used as an argument in a very one-sided manner. Those who categorically maintained corruption in the field of aid was merely a minor problem—and, as long as it was a taboo to speak about corruption, aid sponsors generally belonged to this group—never offered empirical results to justify their reassuring statements. The limited empirical basis not only stems from participants interested in secrecy, thus making corruption more difficult to examine than other social phenomena. The fact that we have few empirically secured data on the extent of corruption in aid results from long-upheld taboos. Methods of accessing data certainly do exist: Development workers and experts working in technical development projects gain so much insight into project realities that they cannot remain ignorant of systematic corruption in those projects in which they are directly involved. That knowledge of corruption phenomena is the subject of everyday conversation among development workers. However, it has not, to my knowledge, ever been systematically gathered or used by aid sponsors. Sponsors keep evaluation reports that hint at misappropriation under lock and key, if such observations are even a part of evaluation requirements. In addition, barriers to the flow of information also exist within sponsoring organizations. Those barriers are discussed in detail in Chapter 9.

Empirical evidence of corruption phenomena manifested itself after the World Bank discarded long-upheld taboos and began researching corruption and its economic and social consequences in developing countries and former communist countries. Household members, corporate managers, and even civil servants have recently been interviewed for empirical studies into the scope and consequences of corruption in their fields.[3] Why should such empirical methods not also be used by aid sponsors, now that they have discarded their a priori claim that their own field was free from corruption, regardless of the environment in which they work? There is hope that the number of serious studies on corruption phenomena in aid will increase following the policy change at the World Bank. The following chapter has also been written with the reservation that empirical research in this field has been neglected. I refer back to my own experience in project work, to confidential memos and informal debate in aid organizations, and to reports available to me.

Corruption in the Phase Prior to Project Approval

In this initial phase, decisions are made regarding how to distribute aid to recipient nations and to recipients inside the respective countries, and which programs and projects shall be further pursued. These choices can be influenced through bribe payments from parties with a vested interest. Such selective decisions are made both in the donor countries and in negotiations between government officials of the donor and recipient countries. Officials in recipient nations have to set the priorities they wish to achieve in negotiation. Little is known about possible pressure through bribery in this selective decisionmaking process. It is conceivable that companies interested in a certain project (for example, a large infrastructure project) pay bribe money to officials in the recipient country or promise to pay if they win a future contract. In doing so, they secure a spot for their preferred project on the list of projects presented to a donor country. One can assume, however, that companies are only willing to pay bribe money during this decisionmaking phase when there is a high probability that they will later be involved in the implementation of a project. There can be no certainty because the final project specifications may not match the services of a company that has paid a bribe, or the procurement process may end up favoring competitors.[4] Only companies with a strong market position in the sector relevant to a project or with close contact to officials in charge of project implementation would thus use financial means to influence officials in the phase prior to project approval.

Decisions made during this phase can also be influenced by another kind of corruption. When officials participating in the decisionmaking process see the possibility of and have an interest in acquiring extralegal income in the ensuing phase of project implementation, they will, based on their own rational thinking, propose projects with the least risk involved for their scheme. Strategies used by officials to limit their risks will be discussed again in the last section of Chapter 5.

Corruption in the Project Implementation Phase

Upon project approval, the type, extent, and site of a project are fixed. Corruption in the next phase occurs in a variety of forms of misappropriation of the means available for project implementation, as well as in the form of bribes with the aim of securing misappropriation.

The Kickback

The kickback is the most important procedure in carrying out misappropriation. As explained earlier, a contractor, in agreement with the client, bills the client more than the usual price—a price above market value or a price higher than the amount that would have been set in a proper procurement process. The contract winner returns all or some of the difference to the officials who granted the contract.

Usually, the officials involved have to manipulate the bidding process in order for the kickback to go through because the supplier cooperating with these officers has to raise the offer by the agreed kickback amount, thus becoming more expensive than the competition. Manipulation of the bidding process can occur in the selection of bidders or in the evaluation of offers, or an agreement to overprice may be reached among bidders to set the stage for a kickback.

The Modified Kickback

In this form of kickback, it is unnecessary to manipulate the bidding process. The price agreed upon corresponds to the market price or is set by a bidding process according to rules. The supplier is nonetheless often pressured into making extralegal payments during project implementation. That kind of pressure can be applied when the contract winner cannot get her partner to fulfill her obligations satisfactorily or when she fears she might be at a disadvantage in later bidding procedures if she refuses to make extralegal payments. The recipients of such payments are either the officials who awarded the contract or officials who can exercise power in the project implementation phase because they inspect the various stages of the project or because they control payments. If extralegal payments were not included in price calculations or in agreements on supplementary charges arising during project implementation, they have to be covered, starting at a certain level, by cuts in project implementation, in particular by a decrease in quality or reduction of the scope of a project.[5]

Making Profits from Project Delays

An external financer generally allocates funds for larger projects in amounts proportionate to the progress made in a project. If there are delays in implementation, funds already disbursed can be invested elsewhere in the meantime. When the profits made from those investments are not returned to project funds but rather pocketed by the people in charge of a project, misappropriation has occurred. In light of high inflation rates and correspondingly high nominal interest rates in a number of recipient countries, this option can be quite lucrative. If financial control is so weak that it is possible for private individuals to pocket profits from such temporary investments, there is an incentive for officials to arbitrarily delay projects.

Returning Goods for Refund

When project implementation requires the distribution of goods purchased with project funds, then goods may be resold and the funds embezzled. Goods are purchased as planned, and thus project managers need not provide false receipts to cover for this type of misappropriation. However, they usually have to manipulate the list of recipients required to prove "proper" distribution of goods. Disaster aid programs that provide for the distribution of goods bought locally or abroad are of relevance to this area.

Manipulating Currency Exchange Rates

Externally provided funds have to be exchanged into the local currency in order to cover costs incurred in the recipient country. Foreign exchange provides an additional possibility for illicit gain in countries that, for whatever reasons, radically intervene in currency transactions, artificially overvalue the local currency, and thus create a black market for foreign exchange. Foreign project funds are exchanged for local currency on the black market at a much more favorable rate than the official one. However, a forged exchange receipt showing the official rate is submitted to the external donor organization. Thus, part of the project money from the black market deal need not be accounted for to the donor. This form of misappropriation is primarily found in the aid projects run by nongovernmental organizations because the people in charge of projects actually exchange the foreign funds themselves.[6]

Using Bribery to Secure Misappropriation

Wherever there are at least rudimentary control mechanisms that restrict misappropriation, officials who embezzle depend on the production of receipts proving "proper" disbursement of funds. Such receipts reduce the risk of being caught but at the same time make misappropriation schemes more difficult to manage. Individual officials or groups of officials working together generally depend on third parties for their success. For example, if officials exchange externally provided funds on the black market, they have to cooperate with bank employees in order to obtain an official receipt of exchange. Falsified distribution lists sometimes have to be signed by third parties. A controlling body has to confirm that a procurement process has been carried out according to rules, when, in fact, certain parts have been manipulated in order to cover for a kickback arrangement. The third parties who assist officeholders with their embezzlement schemes usually also pursue their own financial interests. They will provide an illicit service in exchange for bribe money. In line with the system described in Chapter 2, this is bribery to secure an illegal act. Officials can finance the bribe money paid to third parties with the profits they make through misappropriation. Thus part of the gains from misappropriation is distributed to other civil servants or third parties who are not directly involved in allocating project funds. In cases of systematic corruption, controlling authorities themselves are corrupt, and control mechanisms primarily serve to spread gains from misappropriation beyond the circle of officials who directly exercise discretionary powers over project funds. Under the conditions of systematic corruption, this distribution effect may be an important or even the most important incentive to establish controlling bodies or to work within them.

Nepotism

Decisions regarding the hiring of personnel have to be made during the project implementation phase. If, contrary to any recruitment regulations, the people in charge of hiring give preference to family members, members of their own ethnic group, or people from their home region, then nepotism has occurred. A form of misappropriation can also be connected to nepotism if those favored in the hiring process receive excessive wages for their work, or if they are hired even though project goals could be reached without them. Nepotism can also occur in awarding contracts.

Case Studies

World Bank Projects in Indonesia

Insights into the accumulation of various forms of misappropriation can be found in an internal discussion paper by a group of employees at the World Bank in Indonesia.[7] Their paper provides good insight into corruption in aid projects in a country where corruption is epidemic, like Indonesia. World Bank president Wolfensohn had called for open discussion of the issue of corruption in aid. In 1998 World Bank employees in Indonesia took his request somewhat too seriously. At that time, their paper was not met with undivided enthusiasm at the Bank's central office in Washington, DC. The Indonesian employees rejected the assumption that establishing bodies in the Bank to control corruption might reduce the proportion of embezzled funds in World Bank projects in comparison to all other projects run by the Indonesian government. They quantify that part to be at least 20 to 30 percent. They also point out that the official wages of civil servants in Indonesia lie at the subsistence level, far below the wages of private sector workers with their qualifications, and that the former compensate with side income.[8] Officials have to use a part of their embezzled profits to make good on investments because they were given their positions in exchange for a substantial amount of money or because they are coerced to make campaign donations to the governing political party that they were forced to join.[9] Some of the paper's details about informal payments are given below:

1. Approximately 5 to 10 percent of funds are tagged for informal payments before project implementation begins: among others, payments to planning authorities in order to get a project onto a priority list, or to the ministry of finance in order to secure the disbursement of financial resources that Indonesia is obliged to contribute from its side.

2. Additional informal payments are incurred during the bidding process. The amounts vary greatly, from 5 to 35 percent. They include payments made by interested suppliers who want to be put on the list of approved bidders. If bidders have arranged the outcome of the bidding process among themselves, the bidder designated to "win" pays his or her pretend co-bidders a percentage of the total contract sum (1 to 2 percent per co-bidder). The contract winner is able to secure a contract only by paying the person in charge of the project (who represents a group of officials) a substantial part of the funds through a kickback scheme (approximately 15 percent).[10]

3. Further informal payments are incurred during the project implementation phase. In general, corresponding public offices accept interim reports and pay bills only in exchange for informal payments. Inspectors look for "flaws" in project work, with the intention to demand a fee in exchange for not reporting the flaw (rather than with the intention of improving the situation).

The confidential analysis done by World Bank staff members in Indonesia in 1998 is not outdated. In 2002 the World Bank office in Jakarta and the World Bank Department of Institutional Integrity carried out a fiduciary review of urban development projects funded by the World Bank in cities on the Indonesian island of Sulawesi.[11] It is reasonable to assume that the goals stated in the Bank's Country Assistance Strategy, of fortifying fiduciary controls and reducing corruption in World Bank–financed projects in Indonesia, resulted from the staff members' analysis in the 1998 report. The fiduciary review was hampered by the overwhelming amount of missing documentation for the majority of the contracts—documents relating to the administration of the procurement process and project-related financial information. So it was possible to check only a small number of the procurement packets related to civil works and goods contracts issued in the projects. The main results of the review showed that the procurement process "was manipulated to give [the] appearance of competition. The winners appear to have been pre-selected in most cases."[12] The proof is overwhelming. "Bid prices (total and unit prices) were similar and clustered around the Owner's Estimate almost universally in all contracts in the sample." "In several cases, the arithmetic mistakes in the Owner's Estimate were carried over to the bids." Therefore, the bidders had access to detailed internal price calculations done by the authorities responsible for the projects. Many similarities between the bid proposals of winning and losing bidders "strongly suggest active collusion among bidders." Competing bidders gave the same address; in some cases they even maintained the same bank account. "In many cases, firms from the same ownership cluster were both awarded the contract and had submitted losing bids for the same procurement packet." Participation of "shell" companies was common. Procurement contracts for goods and civil works were split into small lots to limit bidding to companies domiciled in the geographical area of the project. Civil servants responsible for the procurement process maintain a close relationship with those companies. The manipulation of the bidding process was accompanied by weak project implementation. The work performed was not in accordance with the technical specifications included in the contracts. In spite of that, "the actual volumes of works completed were stated in payment documents to be exactly equal to contracted volumes with respect to each sub-component activity." This is unlikely to occur. Because the documentation on project implementation was weak and in some cases nonexistent, the assessment team made site visits. "The contractors and the pimpro [the acronym for the Indonesian project leader] themselves estimated that only 80 percent of the work had been completed." All these results strongly indicate that manipulation of the bidding process was linked to kickbacks in favor of the civil servants responsible for procurement processes and project implementation. Thus this fiduciary review makes clear that the system of corruption in World Bank–financed projects did not change between 1998 and 2002; what changed was the preparedness of the World Bank to investigate. That the results of this investigation are published on the World Bank homepage is a big step forward indeed.

Contract Research as an Instrument for Deviating Funds

The following example is based on my own experience as a project leader in Indonesia.[13] The goal of the project was to establish a research institute. I, as a foreign staff member from a German political foundation, filled the position of research consultant and acted as the counterpart to the Indonesian head of the institute. The institute was to draw up application-oriented studies as one component in founding political decisions, in particular in the area of labor market policies. The institute received research assignments funded by external donors (US aid organizations, among others). Indonesian governmental authorities awarded the research contracts, thus inevitably integrating the whole contract research scheme into the system of primarily illegal side income for public officials. Research contracts were only awarded in cases where the decisionmaking officials could somehow obtain a part of the available funds. One way of doing so was to arrange for feigned consulting. People from the group responsible for awarding contracts were paid a consulting fee without having provided any consulting services. This scheme was essentially nothing but a kickback. Feigned consulting allowed for a bridge between awarding contracts and making side income without anyone having to speak openly about it.[14] Another way of securing embezzlement schemes was the use of title page deals. In this scheme, the research contract was never actually awarded. Instead, a public official wrote the formal text himself, made to look like a real study, and the name of an institute was then bought for 10 to 20 percent of the total contract sum. Title page deals were very unpopular with serious institutes who were forced to publish studies under their name—studies of extremely poor quality, nothing more than bound waste paper. However, they played the game in order to maintain relationships to public officials with discretionary powers over research funds. Then there was the simple kickback with a customary rate of 25 to 30 percent return on the total contract sum. Under such conditions, there should be no illusions about the interest public officials showed in the contents of these studies. Their genuine interest in content would have been a prerequisite for fulfilling the well-meaning goals of the project, namely to contribute to a sound decisionmaking process for forming economic policy. In a few cases, my counterpart negotiated kickback rates for contracts before the topic of the study involved had even been set, a detail so minor for the system of deviating funds.

Disaster Relief in the Bay of Bengal

The coastal regions belonging to India and Bangladesh along the Bay of Bengal are exposed to regularly occurring cyclones and the storm tides that frequently accompany them. There have been several flood disasters accounting for hundreds of thousands of deaths. Due to the dense population and short warning periods, there is no realistic way of evacuating the people from coastal regions in an emergency situation. It is possible, however, to ensure their survival during a cyclone by moving them into shelters. In one single shelter, standing closely together, several thousand people can survive a raging cyclone without injury. The shelters are built of concrete and erected on stilts. The construction of such shelters is the most important disaster prevention program in Bangladesh and the Indian coastal regions along the Bay of Bengal. I had the opportunity to look at such cyclone shelters that had been built under government management. Just a few years after construction, the shelters are in such terrible condition that any further use should be prohibited. Iron beams hang from the ceiling, pieces of concrete are broken off, and the concrete is crumbling. If constructed properly, such shelters should be indestructible and—if adequately maintained—provide protection to the population for many decades. Bearing in mind the mechanisms behind the deviation of funds, it is difficult to accept that failure in this type or similar types of government-run projects is merely a matter of administrative incompetence. It is safe to say that economic calculations underlie most cases. Civil servants or officials of para-governmental organizations accept inadequate building materials and neglect inspections in exchange for a kickback or bribe from the contractor, who gains added income from providing lower quality. Construction of a stable building requires careful supervision. Concrete has to be mixed with sand from fresh-water rivers. What could be more obvious than to reduce high transportation costs and raise profit margins by using the salty sand available for free in coastal regions? It is highly likely that such procedures are at the root of the deterioration of many cyclone shelters built under government supervision on the Indian subcontinent.

Misappropriation in Nongovernmental Organizations

Several additional examples of mismanagement and corruption among nongovernmental organizations (NGOs) are given below:

1. In a West African country, an NGO delegated the customs clearance of foodstuffs imported for an emergency aid program to a company with close connections to the president. That company cleared the goods for a price far above the going rate, which included a blatantly arranged kickback for the head of the nongovernmental organization. Part of the imported powdered milk was routed to dealers who processed it into yogurt and butter candy for the country's middle and upper classes, who have all the purchasing power.
2. One Latin American nongovernmental organization took advantage of hyperinflation at the beginning of the 1990s as a means for deviating funds. In accountability reports to foreign sponsors, staff gave the impression that they had exchanged funds into the local currency immediately after receiving them. In reality, money had been exchanged in small amounts over a longer period of time. They provided blatantly falsified bank receipts to cover themselves. In view of rapidly changing exchange rates in times of hyperinflation, they could make significant gains in the local currency equivalent and did not report a part of the exchange profits to their sponsor.
3. One nongovernmental organization in Asia founded its own intermediate trading organization for delivering large amounts of construction materials to a disaster-stricken region. Staff could thus settle up with their foreign sponsor by providing receipts they produced themselves. The concealed profits were used to create reserves for the organization and to supplement employees' wages.[15]
4. An expatriate staff member of a foreign NGO working in Kosovo handed out a plain application form for a duty exemption

certificate to a local firm. The firm was not a supplier for the NGO; thus there was no legitimate reason for handing out the form. The document enabled the firm to import goods duty-free. The United Nations Mission in Kosovo realized that goods were being imported duty-free without proper reason and imposed a fine on the NGO, as it bore responsibility for the misuse of the form. The NGO staff member's explanation was completely insufficient: He argued that he had been under stress and lacked knowledge about the importance of the duty exemption procedure. He was immediately dismissed, and his former employer forced him to refund part of the damage. This matter was settled out of court.

5. One nongovernmental relief organization operating in Bosnia and Herzegovina realized that the architect working for a returnee housing program funded by this organization took money from the beneficiaries. He succeeded in convincing the beneficiaries that without this payment, they would not have a chance to participate in the program. Beneficiaries were forced to pay between 500 and 1,000 euros.

6. A European NGO supported a sizable NGO in an Asian country in financing relief and development programs in a war-stricken part of the country. Funds were channeled to the headquarters of the NGO in the capital and from there transferred to local branches. The reports sent by the NGO headquarters to the foreign donor were all approved by an auditing firm. At a time when the security situation allowed for field visits, the European donor realized that part of the programs reported had obviously not been implemented. Beneficiaries who were interviewed did not confirm having received the assistance stated in the reports. The donor realized that the elaborately "audited" reports were based on information from the local branches on how they claimed to use the funds to be transferred to them, not on reports of actual expenditure. There had been no auditing of the reports of the branches to the headquarters, which were the basis for the consolidated report to be sent to the foreign donor.

7. The administration of a province in Vietnam obtained financial support from a European NGO for a food-for-work program after a typhoon hit the area. Part of the program involved the repair of an irrigation dam. During a field visit, the donor realized that the existing dam had not been destroyed by the typhoon but had deteriorated mainly from lack of maintenance. The work was carried out by heavy machinery, not by manual labor as indicated in the project document.

The rice funded by the donor had been resold by the administration, and funds were used to rent heavy equipment. The implementation report showed an extent of work much less than what could normally be implemented with the same amount of funding in neighboring countries. The donor was unable to investigate the case and stopped further funding.

8. One European NGO supported an ample food-for-work program run by a local NGO in Afghanistan. The Afghan NGO enjoyed a good reputation because of its capability to balance tensions between different political and ethnic groups in the region. The program intended to support needy landless families and to improve the local infrastructure. Some beneficiaries complained to an Afghan local staff member working for the European NGO that the food distributed was of low quality. He in turn informed his employer, who ordered samples to be collected, which proved the allegation to be true. A firsthand comparison between the prices reported in program documents and market prices led to the assumption that bidding had been manipulated and misappropriation had occurred. When confronted with the allegation, the director of the Afghan NGO argued that long duration of storage and transportation had affected the quality of the food. As to excessive prices, he argued that at the time of purchase food prices were high due to market shortage and that, additionally, the people in the NGO logistics department might have made the mistake of informing the merchants about the food being financed by a European NGO, thus causing prices to be pushed up. The director apologized for any incompetence among his staff. The European NGO then mandated an auditing company to investigate the case. Interviews with merchants did not confirm the alleged market shortage at the time of purchase. Based on a market survey, the auditing company estimated the deviation of actual and reported purchase expenditures to be around US$250,000, approximately one-quarter of total project funds. After this result was presented to the director of the Afghan NGO, he rejected all further communication. Inside the Afghan NGO it was guessed that without the assistance of a local staff member, the European NGO would not have been able to uncover the overpricing. The Afghan staff member of the European NGO who had informed his superior received a warning. Shortly after, he was hit by a car and seriously injured. The driver who caused the accident was the son of a staff member of the Afghan NGO. The European NGO stopped all further funding after having

been informed about overpricing. The public donor of the European NGO refrained from reclaiming its donation because it knew that conditions in Afghanistan are difficult and the recipient aid organization had handled the fraud case and documented it transparently.

Corruption in Violent Conflicts and Postwar Reconstruction

Providing relief aid in violent conflicts is coupled with the risk of aid being transferred to combatants. In extreme cases, aid might prolong conflict. In violent conflicts, conditions make it easy for combatants to confiscate goods without any risk of punishment. A direct transfer of resources also takes place when the transport of relief goods is "taxed": Armed groups allow relief transports to pass only if they receive part of the cargo. Armed groups receive foodstuffs by registering their members or front men as recipients. This occurred in the relief programs for Afghan refugees during and after the Soviet occupation of Afghanistan.

Relief aid can also lead to a transfer of resources in a less direct way. The government of Sudan, engaged in a war against the separation movement in southern Sudan, taxed expenditures made locally by relief organizations by overvaluing its national currency relative to hard currency. The relief organizations were forced to exchange hard currencies into Sudanese currency at a rate up to four times that of the parallel market in order to pay for local expenditures such as transportation, rents, and local personnel. It is believed that the foreign exchange the Sudanese government took in through the big airlift project supported by the UN enabled it at times to cover half of its military expenditures.[16]

As Mary Anderson proved by studying aid programs in conflict situations, relief organizations do have options to counteract attempts by warring factions to get part of the aid provided. Even in conflict situations, relief organizations are not confronted with simple either/or situations: either to provide assistance the way they are accustomed to doing it or to stop aid completely.[17] Rather, relief workers in conflict situations face unique dilemmas. For example, in a situation like that in eastern Zaire in the last weeks of the Mobuto regime, there was no way to know whether one could distribute foodstuffs for refugees and displaced persons while ruling out the possibility that customs people and soldiers got "their share" of the goods, either by means of direct agreements with relief organization representatives or by means of confiscation.[18] Such deals take place in a gray area between corruption and extortion or as the consequence of blunt violence.

Postwar reconstruction seems to take place under more "normal" conditions. Therefore, observers are unsure whether postwar reconstruction provides an extraordinarily tempting setting for large-scale corruption.[19] There are special risks when both the government and the legal system in a postwar situation are still weak. The situation in postwar Bosnia and Herzegovina provides an example of the risks aid programs face. Leading figures of the warring factions were still influential and became the key interlocutors for the international community and the principal entry point into local communities. They often controlled the local market. Aid agencies contracted with cronies of the local elite at inflated prices, while other bidders were warned not to participate in the bidding process for reconstruction contracts.[20] Local leaders can influence a reconstruction program by granting or denying support and legal permission. Vera Devine reports about a nongovernmental organization that had received funding to rebuild houses for returning minorities.

> These leaders might insist that in support for their support, the NGO would undertake a "balancing" project, which they would select. Thus, as well as repairing returnees' houses, NGOs could be coerced into, for example, improving local roads or even assisting local businesses. This had two negative effects: it diverted international funding from the real priorities and strengthened the power of these corrupt local leaders because the majority population believed that they could deliver.[21]

Notes

1. The following portrayal concentrates on project aid in which external sponsors are able to directly influence implementation. The extent to which program aid supporting a wide array of measures (rather than individual projects) and budget aid is affected by corruption is primarily determined by the general level of corruption control in recipient countries.

2. Such dilemmas frequently exist in disaster aid that is provided among the ruins of a fallen political state.

3. See Kaufmann, Pradhan, and Ryterman (1998); Kaufmann (1998); Reinikka and Svensson (2002, 2006).

4. See Holdmann (1997), pp. 61ff.

5. Additional charges arising during project implementation can be justified, for example, by changes in project design. It is in no way certain that a supplier who is forced to make kickback payments will be able to reach an agreement on such supplementary charges at a later point. The supplier faces some risks: The official who awarded the contract in exchange for a bribe might no longer be in charge of the project, or that same official might demand further payments in exchange for an acceptance of additional charges. See Tanzi and Davoodi (1997), p. 7.

6. I know of a few cases in which expatriate project managers have been caught exchanging currency on the black market in countries where, at that time, there was a great difference between the official exchange rate and the black market rate. The temptation to do so is very strong because there are no negative consequences for the project whose interests the leader represents.

7. World Bank Resident Staff, Indonesia (1998).

8. See Cremer (1995), pp. 209–219.

9. The report by World Bank employees refers to the last years of the Suharto government. Suharto stepped down just a few months before the paper was made public. The World Bank reacted by (see Indonesia Daily News Online, August 8, 1998) portraying the report as "outdated," which we can assuredly classify as an attempt to play it down. The World Bank portrayal is not credible for the simple reason that the administration under Suharto's successor Habibie (1998–1999) comprised, in large part, members of the Suharto government. Habibie's administration did not have any fiscal power to reform the pay for civil servants, nor did the succeeding governments: Abdurrahman Wahid, 1999–2001; Megawati Sukarnoputri, 2001–2004; and Susilo Bambang Yudhoyono, since 2004. One can conclude from Transparency International's Corruption Perception Index for 2006 that there have been no fundamental changes in the general situation since the Suharto administration. Indonesia is ranked 130 among 163 countries. Thus, as perceived by informed respondents, Indonesia remains a country with a pronounced level of corruption. See Internet Center for Corruption Research (2006).

10. Kickback amounts vary greatly. For the area of public infrastructure projects run by the ministry of public works, the authors of the report quantify kickback rates in procurement involving international companies at 7 to 12 percent, and procurement involving domestic companies at 12 to 20 percent.

11. World Bank Office, Jakarta (2002), pp. 5ff.

12. Ibid., pp. 5–11.

13. I have documented my experience in detail in Cremer (1990).

14. From my current recollection, it took about one year before I could see through such arrangements. My Indonesian counterpart made arrangements with those in charge of awarding contracts for the institute. In the presence of a foreigner, those arrangements were elaborately disguised.

15. If reserves created in this manner are used for the organization, then the process is not corruption as described earlier in the form of abuse of one's office for private gains. See Chapter 10 of this volume.

16. Duffield (1994), p. 60.
17. Anderson (1999); Anderson (2000).
18. Cremer (1997).
19. Galtung (2005), p. 18.
20. Devine (2005), p. 84.
21. Ibid., pp. 84–85.

5

What Does Corruption Cost?

HOW DO THE CORRUPTION PHENOMENA DESCRIBED EARLIER in this book affect aid projects and the quality and quantity of their intended achievements? From the viewpoint of the Cassen Report, which postulates without proof that corruption affects only a small part of development work, corruption is, at most, a factor that makes aid projects more expensive.[1] Corruption does, of course, raise the costs of development projects and programs. The money that officials directly misappropriate and the bribe payments made to other officials to secure misappropriation constitute funds removed from their proclaimed purpose. It is not possible to draw any general conclusions about what percentage of total project funds are misappropriated. In other words, one cannot determine a general "embezzlement rate." Toward the end of the Suharto era, World Bank staff members quantified this percentage in Indonesia at 20 to 30 percent. This is surely just an estimate made by insiders, but one can assume by well-informed insiders.[2] The share of total project costs arising from corruption in Indonesia has also been quantified by other observers at approximately 30 percent.[3] Public Expenditure Tracking Surveys implemented by the World Bank in Uganda, Tanzania, and Ghana confirm that ghost workers accounted for about 20 percent of total spending, and leakage in nonwage expenditures ranged from 40 to 80 percent.[4]

These numbers represent a striking contradiction to the soothing words of the Cassen Report. Of course, one cannot use these numbers from Indonesia and some African states to make a general statement about development work around the world.[5] It would be rash to generalize because of the current shortage of empirical studies on the problem of corruption in aid work, which resulted from years of sweeping the topic under the carpet. It can be expected that improved empirical data will reveal immense differences between individual recipient countries. The majority of funds are spent via governmental structures in recipient countries. Depending on how potential controlling authorities differ from one country to another—internal administrative controls, the justice system, free press, nongovernmental organizations—the extent of misappropriation of aid funds will also differ.

Corruption makes development projects more expensive, but it is more than merely a factor of cost inflation. It would be appropriate to focus only on inflated costs if a bureaucracy that conducts itself properly spent the same amount of development money on the same programs and projects as its corrupt counterpart. An administration that functions without corruption could, of course, realize a greater number of programs and projects for the same amount of funding because there would be no corruption-based inflation. Other than that, corruption would be inconsequential to the field of development and how it works; everything would simply be more expensive.[6]

The Additional Costs of Corruption

However, the assumption just given is unrealistic. An analysis based solely on data about cost inflation rates caused by extralegal side income for public officials will fall short of its goal. There are many more far-reaching consequences of corruption in the field of aid. To make this clear, it is helpful to take a look at the system of corruption through the vested interests of public officials involved. They run risks whenever they participate in corruption contracts. Public officials have, especially when they act in groups, substantial influence on the terms of the programs they manage. Supervising departments (e.g., ministry of finance) and the managerial staff of an administration depend on detailed knowledge when formulating policies and programs. However, only the officials working in a certain area actually possess that detailed knowledge. There is every reason for us to assume that public officials use the decisionmaking scope in their specialized field to minimize the risks of corrupt behavior and to influence budget allocation in such a way that improves their chances of gaining extralegal income.

A Tendency Toward Large-Scale Projects

In order to gain income through misappropriation, it is necessary to have direct or indirect right of disposal of budget decisions. It is plausible that officials are able to embezzle a certain amount of money with fewer risks in a large project than in a smaller project.[7] Rational corrupt officials will consequently fight for the largest piece of the budget they can possibly get to fulfill their tasks. As is known, officials in bureaucracies where corruption is not a widespread phenomenon also fight for big pieces of the budget because their status and powers of influence are connected to the right of disposal of the budget. However, in administrations where systematic corruption reigns, the fight for more funding is heightened by an immediate material interest on the part of officials.

Such material interests also influence the decision to carry out a project at all. It is the duty of public officials to check whether a project corresponds to the priorities set, for example, in a development plan. If people who directly or indirectly participate in a misappropriation scheme check a project for its relevance to a development policy, one cannot expect there to be any restrictions on spending as a result of that check. Starting at a certain project size, the administrative unit directly responsible for executing a project commonly must gain approval on their decisions. Approval by a supervising administrative unit, such as the ministry of finance or planning authorities, is usually required. However, the approval system can have a controlling effect only if the supervising body itself does not profit from embezzled funds. Lists drawn up by the World Bank staff in Indonesia during the Suharto era include planning authorities and the ministry of finance as recipients of extralegal payments to be made during individual project phases.[8] Such payments are essential in getting the project on a priority list and in having funds disbursed. A priority check does not necessarily contradict the private interests of officials in a supervising body, as long as the rejection of one project frees up financing for another project that provides for the same amount of side income earned by corrupt practices. However, as soon as rejection of one project leads to a reduction of funds to be spent or controlled within their own realm—a reduction because a higher-priority project falls into the lap of other officials—then a truly critical priority check contradicts the interests of corrupt officials. All things considered, it is plausible that the decision regarding the priority and scale of a project may "turn out more expensive" in corrupt administrations than in administrations where corruption control works effectively. In extreme cases, the decision to carry on with a project is made simply because those in charge intend to embezzle the respective funds.

Which Expense Items Are "Misappropriation-Friendly"?

The calculations of corrupt public officials can also influence decisions about how available funds are allocated to individual budget items. One can assume that, where embezzlement amounts are constant, the risk related to different types of budget items varies. Certain procedures for deviating funds have to be followed in order to set up a complete financial report that makes it appear no embezzlement has occurred (see Chapters 2 and 7 in this book).

A corresponding expenditure is recorded in the books to cover for corrupt activity. This fake entry is comparatively easy in investment projects because misappropriation can be secured through a kickback. The problem of producing receipts is shifted from public officials to their suppliers. Misappropriating funds from personnel budgets, however, entails more risks because it reduces payments for employees who usually know exactly what they should get. This is an important reason for the poor maintenance and quick deterioration of public infrastructure facilities in numerous developing countries. Periodic new investments constitute large-scale projects, within which the potential for kickback arrangements is obvious. Regular maintenance work, by contrast, which would prolong the life cycle of infrastructure facilities and diminish the need for new investments, incurs personnel costs that have little potential for misappropriation.[9] A rationally acting corrupt official would thus use his or her sphere of influence to make sure that, during the budget planning phase, expense items are given priority based on their potential for misappropriation with the least possible risk.

Disastrous Results of the Modified Kickback

In a modified kickback scheme, a contract has been awarded at fair market price. However, suppliers are forced to make informal payments to the awarding officials throughout contract execution. Money for these informal payments can be obtained by reducing the size of a project or by lowering its quality standards. Often, additional bribe money then must be paid to controlling authorities responsible for adherence to contract stipulations. A modified kickback scheme can have particularly disastrous consequences if suppliers compensate for the illegal payments they are forced to make by lowering quality standards (for example, using inferior building materials). Infrastructure investments are clearly the main focus of financial cooperation. One characteristic of infrastructure investments is the ease with which quantity can be increased at the expense of quality.[10] Even in adhering to the quantitative scope used to calculate costs and fixed in a project plan, substantial extralegal income can be made at the expense of quality and life cycle. Indonesians say, "Public officials eat asphalt," when referring to the connection between extralegal income and the poor quality of their streets. The sad condition of many cyclone shelters built under government supervision along the Bay of Bengal, as described in Chapter 4, is most likely a consequence of modified kickback schemes.

Increasing the Complexity of Decisionmaking Processes

Experience with project work in developing countries has shown that decisionmaking processes are often complex and time-intensive. Often it is not even possible to adequately check which offices are responsible for what. Nearly every aid worker and expert who takes on work in a developing country is confronted with these facts and usually undergoes culture shock for this and for other reasons. For those who are not familiar with an environment of epidemic corruption, it is a natural reaction to blame frustrating circumstances on the incapability or disinterest of public officials. However, the complexity of decisionmaking processes may very well be the natural result of self-interest on the part of rationally acting officials. Participation in decisionmaking or control procedures secures participation in embezzled funds. Big steering committees enlarge the circle of people participating in misappropriated gains. Officials of supervising bodies such as planning authorities can delay work and enhance their chances of receiving bribe money by requiring their subordinate offices to get approval on all details of project implementation. Such mechanisms help to distribute misappropriated gains from the hands of officials directly involved in allocating budget money and in a position to arrange a kickback, into the hands of officials who would otherwise not participate and be left to rely on their legal wages.

The self-interest of corrupt public officials affects projects in the following ways: (1) a tendency toward large-scale projects and a preference for "embezzlement-friendly" project designs; (2) a reduction in the life cycle of infrastructure facilities due to modified kickbacks; and (3) a tendency toward complex decisionmaking processes, which are also related to higher costs. Because of these tendencies, the total costs incurred by misappropriation are in general significantly higher than the misappropriated gains made by participating decisionmakers. When a project is implemented for the sole reason of deviating funds, then all project expenses must be classified as costs incurred by corruption. Additional social costs arising during implementation of a project used to secure the deviation of funds—social costs such as population resettlement or environmental damage—must also be considered costs incurred by corruption. Occasionally, corruption is believed to be an alternative form of paying civil servants' wages. However, for the general public, that is a costly way to increase inadequate salaries in the public sector.

Who Is Being Hurt?

Corruption in development projects harms those who do not receive any intended aid at all or who receive aid of poorer quality or at a later date than intended. Corrupt public officials who are aware of risks need to consider the potential for resistance among the people hurt by their behavior. The potential for resistance is primarily a question of organization and political influence. People without this leverage are less likely to be taken into account as recipients of public services, even by a legally operating administration, than their well-organized and politically influential compatriots. They are also more likely to become victims of embezzlement schemes. In their attempt to quantify misappropriation rates, the Indonesian World Bank staff estimated the portion of funds deviated from compensation money for people who had to be resettled to make way for large projects at 50 to 80 percent. This number is much higher than the 20 to 30 percent the World Bank staff members consider a realistic average for all development programs in Indonesia.[11] This discrepancy is no coincidence. Victims of forced resettlement had few possibilities—especially during the repressive Suharto era—of fighting for their compensation, either in court or through political pressure.

Following the same logic, misappropriation in public spending for social programs first affects those who are poor and have no political influence, those who are primarily dependent on public services because they cannot obtain educational or health services on the free market.[12] Multiple-country analysis of the relationship between corruption perception indexes and indicators of the provision of health care and education services shows that a high level of corruption has adverse consequences for a country's child and infant mortality rates and dropout rates in primary schools.[13]

Looking Through the Eyes of Government Officials

Development aid workers, especially those new to the field, will happen upon incidents that seem odd, even absurd, from their point of view. They will look for explanations. Every newcomer will first blame such unpleasant phenomena on administrative incompetence, inadequate qualification, or lack of motivation on the part of public officials. It would do a newcomer good in furthering his or her experience to try to look at seemingly odd occurrences from the perspective of a rationally acting official who wants to gain extralegal income at a risk or who, if crassly underpaid, has to do so to survive.

I was able to understand certain phenomena from my own project work as a research consultant in Indonesia only after I had learned to assume this point of view. Why would a ministry award a research contract on a particular topic, even though a contract with a similar or identical focus was awarded just a few years ago?[14] Why is no information on former studies passed onto the new contract winners? Old studies have, possibly, simply been forgotten. But even if someone remembered them and they already contained the information expected from the new study, there would be no cause to refrain from awarding a new contract if the public officials in charge were interested in making side income from bogus consulting or kickback arrangements. Or how can it be that one government authority simultaneously awards two identical contracts, one to a foreign consultant and one to an Indonesian research institute, and that apparently nobody is interested in bringing the two together? They may not even find out the other exists until they are coincidentally meeting at a closing seminar. The foreign consultant is generally paid directly by the foreign donor organization sponsoring the project. Misappropriation by public officials in the recipient country is basically out of the question in that case. Therefore, one cannot help suspecting that the parallel contract with the Indonesian research institute was, for the most part, included in project planning in order to create one component that leaves room for the usual deviation of funds. One final example: Why would one ministerial department be so determined to build an electronic data bank and data-processing system when the required initial data for such a system are not even available, and when it is not clear what administrative purposes the system would serve or what questions it would answer? Their determination could simply represent a naive belief in the possibilities a centralized database offers to planning. However, again, one cannot help but think that other factors play a role; namely, that the type of large-scale investment necessary for building such a system eases the way for getting kickback payments with little risk.

Notes

1. Cassen (1986), p. 13.
2. This estimate is supported by details regarding payments made to public officials during individual project phases. Respective ranges for the percentage of embezzled funds during individual project phases add from 13.5 to 75 percent of the total budget. See World Bank Resident Staff, Indonesia (1998); Bosshard (1998).
3. Jeffrey Winters, *Far Eastern Economic Review,* February 13, 1997 (quoted in Bosshard 1998), and the doyen of Indonesian economists and former finance minister, Sumitro Djojohadikusumo (see Caufield 1997, p. 246).
4. World Bank (2002a), p. 22.
5. There is also no plausible reason to consider Indonesia an isolated case, however. The Corruption Perception Index of 1997 ranked Indonesia 46 among 52 countries, at an index score of 2.72 (0 = observers view the country as completely corrupt; 10 = observers view the country as completely free from corruption). In the Corruption Perception Index of 2006, Indonesia was ranked 130 of 163 countries, with a score of 2.4. In both years, Indonesia had scores similar to those of other important recipient countries involved in development work. See Internet Center for Corruption Research (1997, 2006).
6. In countries where underpaid public officials enhance income with extralegal sources, the net effect of corruption-based cost inflation in aid programs is lower than the gross effect. They would have to be legally paid better wages when improved corruption control is in place.
7. Assuming control procedures have not substantially been stepped up because of the project's size.

8. See World Bank Resident Staff, Indonesia (1998).

9. See World Bank (1987), pp. 65ff. In principle, it would be conceivable to award maintenance contracts to external companies and to use contract negotiations for kickback arrangements. Maintenance would then no longer represent a conflict of interests for corrupt public officials. For empirical correlations between corruption and the poor quality of public infrastructure investments, see Tanzi and Davoodi (1997), pp. 17–18; Tanzi and Davoodi (1998), pp. 9–10.

10. Frey (1978), p. 201.

11. World Bank Resident Staff, Indonesia (1998).

12. See, for example, the results of Public Expenditure Tracking Surveys in education: Reinikka and Smith (2004), pp. 74ff, 93ff.

13. Gupta, Davoodi, and Tiongson (2000), p. 24.

14. The following examples are from Cremer (1990), pp. 220–221.

6

Corruption Control as a Global Responsibility

THOSE WHO DEAL WITH CORRUPTION SPECIFICALLY IN developing countries run the risk of neglecting the global context of this phenomenon. Corruption would then appear to be primarily or even exclusively a phenomenon that plagues developing countries. Because of this very risk, debate about the phenomenon of corruption in developing countries was long subject to an intellectual ban, in particular within aid institutions themselves. It violated the rules of political correctness to talk about corruption in developing countries and in aid without at the same time mentioning corruption in the administrations of industrial countries and qualifying the effects of corruption in developing countries by pointing out other, especially external, factors that inhibit development. As important as it is to analyze a social phenomenon in its surrounding context, the pressure to qualify was much greater in discussing the phenomenon of corruption than in discussing other issues. The reason for such unequal treatment was presumably the fact that corruption phenomena force us in a special way to take a look at the accountability behind obstacles to development processes, accountability found with the political elite in developing countries. Their behavior arouses doubts about how sensible it is to transfer aid funds when the lion's share flows to the political elite. For a long time, the development community wanted to avoid such doubts, supposedly to defend the interests of international solidarity and to preserve the willingness on the part of industrial nations to provide financing to developing countries. However, this attitude of avoidance impeded a differentiated view of accountability for a long time.

There is another impediment to viewing corruption control as a global imperative. Many people believe that corruption is deeply rooted in the cultures of developing countries. If that were the case, the battle against corruption would end up in a clash of cultures, and a global partnership would be difficult to establish.

Corruption Cannot Be Explained in Predominantly Cultural Terms

This section is a brief aside serving to support my firm position that the widespread existence of corrupt behavior among officials in developing countries should not be considered a phenomenon predominantly explainable in cultural terms.

So-called antimoralists who sharply criticize those who apply "Western" norms to "non-Western" societies make a point that is partly justified. The term *corruption* can only apply when the behavior of an official contradicts the norms of his or her society. We can only really talk about bribery when the acceptable norms of a certain society characterize the purchase of favors in courts or administrations as unjust. Talk of misappropriation of public means requires a clear distinction between the means officials manage as part of their official duties and their private assets. But if the role of public officials had no legal definition, if there were no limits to their discretionary powers, if there were no separation between government property and an official's personal belongings, nothing would stand in the way of public officials filling their private coffers with national wealth. As imperfectly as norms for public office are enforced, without such a legal framework the governments of today's developing countries could not function. There is a distinction between public and private spheres, and there are norms either put forth by law or anchored in social consensus that govern the behavior of public officials. Therefore, the requirements have been met for using the term *corruption* in reference to the conduct of people holding office.

The so-called antimoralists also often accuse those who make an issue of corruption in non-Western societies of neglecting cultural factors in discussing what they call corruption. The norms established by society that determine whether the conduct of public officials is legitimate or corrupt cannot be truly understood without taking cultural peculiarities into consideration. One simple point, however, argues against defining corruption as a predominantly cultural problem. We observe bribery, misappropriation, and nepotism in societies of extremely divergent cultural character, in Latin America, strongly influenced by Christianity, as well as in Islamic societies, in sub-Saharan Africa as well as in the countries of southern and Southeast Asia. Therefore, those who explain corruption in predominantly cultural terms should have to explain why extremely divergent cultural traditions lead to such similar phenomena. Corruption was also widespread in the communist societies of Eastern Europe; the control mechanisms of civil society were crushed with the establishment of single-party rule, or, in the case of the Soviet Union, civil control mechanisms were never able to unfold.[1] A cultural explanation of corruption is also hardly compatible with the fact that Singapore and Hong Kong have succeeded in curbing corruption despite cultural traditions very similar to those in other countries of that region where such successes have not been possible.[2]

Further observations are also difficult to reconcile with the cultural point of view, namely that what Western critics call corruption may be widely accepted conduct in non-Western societies. In nearly every case of undemocratic seizure of power, the new rulers try to justify the change by accusing their fallen predecessors of corruption. In established democracies the issue of corruption is of central importance in the competition among political parties. For my argument, it is completely irrelevant whether a new government, in power either by putsch or election, makes any progress in controlling corruption. What is relevant is the sheer fact that the new rulers find it opportune to accuse their predecessors of corruption. That alone proves that the population expects people in public office to behave in a certain way. Censorship often targets media that not only discuss bribery, misappropriation, and nepotism in a very general sense, but that also look into and publish concrete cases in the form of investigative journalism. The political joke, an important reflection of prevalent opinions in countries in which the population is not allowed to articulate its views via independent organizations or a free press, is full of subtle allusions to all facets of corruption. Such occurrences show that broad parts of society have developed standards defining legitimate conduct in public office, and that the behavior of officials is measured against these norms and, in certain situations, found to be corrupt. That means Western critics of corruption refer to values and norms found not only in their own culture but also in non-Western societies.[3]

That does not mean that certain types of behavior are always evaluated equally. The line between correct conduct and corrupt conduct can be drawn differently in different societies, and cultural factors can, of course, play a large role in drawing that line. In assessing an actual type of behavior, one can judge whether an abstract principle has been violated or whether personal harm has been done. A violation of accepted norms for public office that occurs with the intention of fulfilling conflicting values and norms can be assessed differently in differing societies. Family solidarity is one such type of conflicting value. It results in the obligation to stand by relatives in dire situations. The traditional duty, as seen in Southeast and East Asia, of recording the quality of a relationship by exchanging gifts, leads to gift exchanges in negotiations and to an occurrence that guidelines in Western countries attempt to prevent.[4] There is, however, a distinct difference between a gift on the one hand and a bribe on the other. A gift is given with the intention of maintaining a social relationship. The giver expects a return gift at some undetermined future time, whereas the briber wants immediate payback.[5] In Southeast and East Asia people clearly recognize when a bribe is "performed under the banner of the gift mechanism to exploit its social characteristics and disguise its own illegitimacy."[6] A distinction between the official sphere and the private sphere that is accepted in principle can be interpreted with varying degrees of precision.[7] Differences based on culture are of central importance to every strategy of corruption control. Ignoring these differences can lead to major misjudgments, especially in development aid, where members of different cultures work together. But, once again, the fact that the line of distinction between correct and corrupt conduct may be drawn differently in different countries should not lead us to believe that the term *corruption* is not transferable to non-Western countries.

Corruption as a Global Phenomenon

Corruption is a global phenomenon, thus making corruption control a shared responsibility among industrial and developing countries. Corruption can be found worldwide, just like other forms of crime. Simple economic models that tease out the calculations of those deciding whether to act in a corrupt or in a correct manner can explain why corruption is a global phenomenon. Such models also show why levels of corruption vary among different societies without pointing to cultural factors and without stigmatizing certain societies by implicitly assuming their ethics are underdeveloped.

One simplified—but in this context useful—economic approach is based on an individual who is pursuing his own interests and who intends to maximize his gains under the conditions provided by an existing institutional framework. On the basis of his individual utility calculation, this person decides how to conduct himself, whether corruptly or correctly, and, if corruptly, what strategy he shall pursue. If he has no purely inner motivation, such as religion or ethical values, his adherence to norms is based solely on the threat of a penalty for deviant behavior.[8] This approach is, of course, extremely simplified because there are indeed inner mechanisms that can cause a person to act in compliance with societal norms and to forgo infringement that would enrich him, even if he need not fear apprehension or negative consequences. However, this approach can explain under which conditions incentives arise for individuals to act in a corrupt manner.

The simple approach of such a model captures the calculations done by active and passive partners in a bribe with very few variables.[9] Bribery is, as portrayed here, an exchange. One partner, usually described as the active party, pays a bribe to an official, the passive party, who then breaks with norms to guarantee an illegal service in exchange. Both partners will enter into the exchange only when they are convinced by their individual calculations that the exchange is worthwhile, in other words, that the gains made through bribery are greater than the costs. In doing their calculations, they will at least consider the following variables: What is the value of the bribed service, or how great is the difference between the gains made by the active party in the case of a bribe and the gains made via the best legal alternative? How much will it cost to acquire the information needed to set up a bribe contract? What is the likelihood of the bribe being exposed because of the risks involved in looking for a partner willing to enter a bribe? What if a third party reports the bribe to the police, a third party who suffers damages because of the bribe? What penalties would the bribe partners have to reckon with? Incentives to enter a bribe situation always arise when the calculation variables reach a level that makes the bribe worthwhile for both parties, when the maximum amount the active party is willing to offer exceeds the minimum amount the passive party would have to demand in order to cover his costs.

From this point of view, it is completely plausible to characterize corruption as a global phenomenon. Incentives to bribe are always especially large whenever officials can offer services of high value and, at the same time, risks are low or expected penalties insignificant. If these conditions are met in industrial nations, corruption becomes a widespread problem there as well. It is no coincidence that some of the biggest corruption scandals in industrial countries have occurred in the field of arms production: The value of bribed services, such as the elimination of a public procurement process that limits pricing possibilities for suppliers, is extremely high. There is a broad decisionmaking scope for fixing prices on complex arms products because they lack the price comparison possibilities found among standard mass-produced goods. Therefore, control costs are high, and the risk of corrupt arrangements being exposed is low. When political patronage comes into play, the risk of punishment drops even further. The differences between industrial and developing nations in the spread of corrupt practices can be fully explained by diverse values attached to the above-mentioned calculation variables. It is those values that result in different levels of incentives for corrupt practices.

Corruption in International Economic Relations

Corruption is not only a worldwide phenomenon but also a crime that often accompanies global cooperation. Corruption in international economic relations is committed by active parties, both in industrial and in developing countries. With corruption in developing countries, the key to changing calculation variables, and thus reducing incentives for corrupt practices, lies with the political and legal institutions of the developing countries, but with corruption in international economic relations, partial responsibility lies directly with the governments of industrial nations. This is of great significance when looking at the issue of how to control corruption in aid because a big part of funds for financial aid are used to purchase goods from industrial countries.

The governments of most industrial nations shirked this responsibility for a long time. Only the United States was willing, in 1977, to make the bribery of foreign officials a punishable offense.[10] With that, the United States helped to change the calculation variables for corrupt parties in such a way that their incentives were diminished.

Since then decisionmakers in US businesses who secure foreign contracts with bribes have risked prosecution. The governments of other important industrial nations were not only unwilling to follow the US example, but they even designed their tax laws to encourage corruption in international business deals. Until the passage of the tax law of March 24, 1999, German tax authorities were required to classify bribes paid in foreign countries under "useful expenditures" so that they were tax-deductible. The corresponding enactment read: "Tax authorities shall waive the receipt requirement for payments to foreign recipients when it has been established that the payment was made within the framework of a usual business partnership, that the amount paid flowed into a foreign country, and that the recipient is not subject to German tax laws."[11] This regulation constituted a direct share of responsibility for corruption in developing countries and for the misuse of aid funds. With tax benefits for bribe payments and no threat of prosecution, the law amounted to an instrument for promoting corrupt exports at the cost of competitors who were not willing to pay bribe money. The German tax regulation caused outrage, especially in the United States, where business partners risked criminal prosecution if they tried to bribe foreign officials. The German federal government long refused to abolish the regulation allowing for tax deduction of bribe payments made abroad. This refusal was, at the same time, crassly inconsistent with policies toward developing countries.[12] Tolerating bribery in defense of international competition and bearing responsibility for bribes made to officials in developing countries were not compatible with the hypocritical demands placed on developing country partners to promote competition and good governance. Developing countries responded to this inconsistency in an appropriately malicious manner.

The common practice among export nations of bribing officials in developing countries in order to prevail in the struggle for contracts is reflected in the Bribe Payers Index (BPI), published by Transparency International since 1999. (Since 1995 Transparency International has also published the Corruption Perception Index, which ranks countries based on the perceived spread of corruption in public service.)[13] The Bribe Payers Index categorizes the leading export nations according to their willingness to pay bribes. The 2006 index ranked thirty leading export nations according to the propensity of firms with headquarters within their borders to bribe when operating abroad. More than 11,000 business executives from companies in

125 countries were asked to identify the country of origin of foreign-owned companies doing the most business in their country and then to answer the following question: "In your experience, to what extent do firms from the countries you have selected make undocumented extra payments or bribes?" The respondents were asked to answer on a scale of 1 (= bribes are common) to 7 (= bribes never occur). Some important export nations, including the United States, the UK, and Germany, were ranked in the cluster of countries from which companies are least likely to bribe, but even for these countries the respondents gave ratings that show a considerable propensity to bribe.[14]

Only since the mid-1990s have the governments of industrial countries begun to show a willingness to take on some responsibility for corruption control in international commerce. At the urging of the Organization for Economic Cooperation and Development (OECD), they signed a convention on December 17, 1997, regarding bribery of foreign officials in international business dealings. The agreement obliges them to prosecute the bribery of officials abroad if the bribe aims to secure a contract in an international business deal or to obtain any other unjust advantage.[15] Influencing a procurement procedure by arranging for a kickback definitely falls into this category of bribe. The convention went into effect on February 15, 1999, and, in Germany, has been integrated into the law against international bribery. Tax laws have also been adapted. The outrageous regulation allowing for deduction of bribe payments made abroad has been abolished.

The OECD convention is an important step toward fighting bribery in international trade, but the impact of this convention and the national laws created in its wake depend on the seriousness of the implementation process on the national level in the industrialized countries that dominate international trade. The empirical analysis of the data emerging from the 2004 Executive Opinion Survey (EOS) of the World Economic Forum conveys insight into the gap between the spirit of the convention and reality. The data show that, according to the perception of the respondents, transnationals headquartered within OECD countries but operating in non-OECD countries exhibit much lower (often illegal) corporate ethical standards in the latter; their behavior is often more similar, in fact, to that of domestic firms in the recipient country.[16] Given the corruption found in governments in both developing and fast-developing nations, it will remain very tempting for businesses to employ bribe payments in the fight for contracts. At the same time, it is tempting for the governments of industrial nations to tolerate bribe payments as a means of promoting exports, in particular when they expect that competitors in other countries are also making bribe payments, despite the OECD agreement.[17] The convention and its corresponding national laws can only bear fruit with the active involvement of prosecuting authorities and the establishment of a system of mutual assistance in international law enforcement. Only then can businesses defend themselves when they have not been selected in a procurement process due to the fact that competitors were willing to pay a bribe.

The OECD convention would be much more effective if national law punished not only an individual caught bribing in order to secure a contract for his company but also the organization of which he is a member. The board of directors of a company often bears partial responsibility, either because they neglected to establish effective controls or because they encouraged employees to act as they did for the good of the company. If it were possible in all countries to punish the organization's failure in addition to prosecuting the direct offender, there would be greater incentive for companies to prevent their staff from paying bribes. In a liability case involving the organization, a company would have to account to the court for its part in controlling corruption if it wanted to fend off court sanctions.[18]

One Cannot *Not* Intervene!

The implementation of the OECD initiative is important to development aid. But controlling corruption in international relations is not only the duty of people active in international commerce. People involved in aid programs also bear direct responsibility. Aid funds constitute one of the sources of corrupt income for officials in developing countries. If aid workers do not use the possibilities available to them to restrict corruption, then they are directly accountable. It is still difficult for many aid organizations to face the responsibility of corruption control. Many of them have not yet overcome the subliminal feeling that demanding precise agreement on how funds are disbursed is a form of unreasonable meddling. However, each and every form of aid constitutes intervention in the "internal affairs" of a partner country, in part because of the inevitable decision as to which programs should foster which institutions and groups. Therefore, for those foreign aid employees who still have reservations about taking on responsibility for corruption control—just as Paul Watzlavick, Janet H. Beavin, and Don D. Jackson said, people cannot *not* communicate—in the field of foreign project sponsorship, the active parties cannot *not* intervene.[19]

Notes

1. On corruption in communist systems, compare, for example, Voslensky (1985) and Kramer (1977/1999). On corruption in postsocialist countries, see Varese (1997); Grødeland, Koshechkina, and Miller (1998); and Anderson and Gray (2006).

2. See case studies in Klitgaard (1988), pp. 98ff (Hong Kong), and pp. 122ff (Singapore); Shang (2002), pp. 51ff (Hong Kong), and pp. 124ff (Singapore); De Speville (1997); and Quah (1999).

3. At any rate, Indonesian intellectuals in my acquaintance did not understand my attempts to discuss the question of the transferability of the term *corruption* to a society like Indonesia because they had no doubts at all that their government is corrupt.

4. Leisinger (1997), pp. 69ff.

5. Verhezen (2002), p. 60.

6. Ibid., p. 58; compare also Gransow (1991), pp. 346ff. See also Klitgaard (1988), pp. 62ff, on gift mechanisms in African societies.

7. A few years ago the German media played up a scandal surrounding Rita Süßmuth, then German parliamentary president. It centered on world-shattering issues such as whether President Süßmuth's husband was entitled to be driven home in his wife's official car in order to change clothes for an official occasion at which he was to accompany his wife. Germany's close neighbors, the Italians, would have probably just shaken their heads over that "scandal."

8. Richter and Furubotn (2003), pp. 2ff; Furubotn and Richter (2005).

9. See Neugebauer (1978), pp. 15ff; Borner and Schwyzer (1999), pp. 21ff, with regard to bribery.

10. Foreign Corrupt Practices Act (FCPA), December 19, 1977.

11. Enactment to Abgabenordnung (tax code) No. 1977 of September 24, 1987, BStBl. I, 664 of § 160 clause 4. See also Kreppel (1995), p. 33.

12. Leisinger (1997), pp. 79–80.

13. The Corruption Perception Index combines approximately ten corruption indexes ascertained primarily for use in consulting internationally active companies. People with regional knowledge, such as local businesspeople and employees of multinational companies, as well as businesspeople and experts from foreign countries, are asked how they rate the level of corruption in the respective country (0 = considered by observers to be completely corrupt; 10 = considered by observers to be free from corruption). The high correlation among different indexes leads to the conclusion that there is a certain level of agreement among observers as to how they classify

countries with regard to the spread of corruption. See Lambsdorff (1999a), pp. 300ff; Internet Center for Corruption Research (2002, 2006), in particular "Frequently asked questions."

14. In calculating the BPI, the answers were converted to a score between 0 and 10. Some examples of the average score and standard deviation for selected countries: UK 7.39/2.67; Germany 7.34/2.74; United States 7.22/2.77; France 6.50/3.00; Russia 5.16/3.34. See Transparency International (2006).

15. The sole fact that a foreign officer has been offered a bribe is decisive in determining whether a punishable offense has been committed. The following aspects, among others, are of no significance: the value of gains, whether the bribe was successful, knowledge about local practices, or tolerance of such payments by local authorities. Not included in the agreement are smaller payments to make business easier, that is, payments made in order to get officials to do their jobs (e.g., the issuance of permits). The term *official* is broadly described and includes people who work in public companies. "Public companies" are, regardless of their legal form, businesses directly or indirectly ruled by the public hand (through, for example, a majority stake in capital or majority representation on the supervisory board). See also the commentary accompanying the agreement. The convention and its accompanying commentaries are documented in OECD (2000), pp. 243ff. Compare also Pieth (1999), pp. 344ff.

16. Kaufmann (2004), pp. 92–93.

17. See Goudie and Stasavage (1997), p. 16.

18. Sacerdoti (1999), pp. 221–222; Schauenberg (2000), pp. 404ff.

19. Watzlawick, Beavin, and Jackson (1968).

7

Is Corruption Control a Lost Cause?

EVEN THOUGH DEVELOPMENT AID ORGANIZATIONS DO NOT like talking about the extent to which their funds form the basis of extralegal income for public officials, the topic is certainly not unknown to them. Control regulations are derived from the budget stipulations commonly seen in Western industrialized countries. All development aid organizations have to fulfill those stipulations, both the state authorities involved in bilateral cooperation as well as the nongovernmental organizations that receive financing from public funds. NGOs also adhere to control regulations about allocating funds from their own coffers or from private donations, even if less strictly than when spending public funds tied to the specifications of the financing party. At the core of regulation lies the obligation to account for all expenditures in writing as well as to award large-scale contracts on the basis of a procurement process.

The Production of Receipts

In countries where corruption is an everyday phenomenon, regulations provide much less protection against misappropriation of project funds than, for example, in the United States or Germany. In order to minimize their risks, public officials in developing countries put a substantial amount of creative energy into making a formal and correct impression by producing false receipts to cover misappropriation, using elaborate methods to do so. There is a difference here between internal procedures within administrations on the one hand,

and procedures that require cooperation with outside parties on the other.

Internal Procedures Within Administrations

In this case, an individual or a group of officials produces receipts that conceal misappropriation and make it look as though funds have been properly allocated. For example, officials may (1) falsify recipient lists to conceal the embezzlement of materials or money meant to be distributed to beneficiaries; (2) add fictitious workers to payrolls; (3) force staff members to sign papers saying that they have received more pay than they actually have; or (4) bill for administrative costs that were never incurred, such as fictitious business trips. When I was working in development in Indonesia, it was possible to buy the stub of a plane ticket for 5 to 10 percent of the regular price. Civil servants from Jakarta could use them to "account for" a business trip to the province. According to some insiders I have spoken with, the provincial administration officials who, on paper, had had a visitor, usually would confirm that visit when requested. Civil servants in the province depend on cooperation with their colleagues in the capital city. They were probably reluctant to hinder cover-up schemes because their doing so could result in less funding for their own areas of responsibility, which served, in turn, as the basis of illegal side income in the provinces. Where there is only very weak external control, it is also possible to simply falsify receipts.

Producing Receipts in Cooperation with Third Parties

Misappropriation that can be secured through internal procedures within an administration is, at least if rudimentary internal accounting controls are in place, limited in its scope. Therefore, officials employ additional cover-up procedures involving cooperation with outside parties. In many countries, it is a part of customer service for suppliers to issue excessive invoices with which the embezzlement of project funds can be concealed. Corrupt officials can increase the willingness of suppliers to cooperate in such schemes by threatening them with the loss of a contract or telling them they will not be considered for future contracts. The kickback procedure for covering up embezzlement also requires cooperation with third parties. Kickbacks have an inestimable advantage for officials because the problem of accounting for the misappropriated sum shifts to the contract winner. There is no numerical evidence of a kickback in the bookkeeping records of an official because the disbursement of funds is accounted for in the overpriced invoice.

The Manipulation of Bidding Procedures

As shown earlier, when a kickback is used to secure a misappropriation scheme, the price has to exceed the usual so that the contract winner can use the excess to finance the return payment she owes to an official. However, for contracts starting at a certain value (fixed by control regulations), public officials are not able to set the price of a contract themselves. Rather, they are bound to a tendering procedure. In such cases, securing a kickback entails manipulating a tendering procedure at the same time.

Tendering procedures are indispensable in controlling how public contracts, including aid contracts, are awarded.[1] Market prices can often be established only with difficulty or sometimes not at all because the government itself is the sole client or because certain specifics of a contract make it impracticable to draw comparisons with other contracts. A lack of economic efficiency in procurement processes generally does no harm either to government officials or to project managers and staff. The target groups of aid projects bear the brunt alone. Tendering procedures are meant to force bidders into "organized competition," ensuring the economic efficiency of procurement and, through objectivity, maintaining the principle of equal treatment of all bidders.

Different processes are possible. In an *open tender,* the call for bids is open to an unlimited number of companies, thus allowing for competition from newcomers. In a *restricted tender,* the client invites selected companies to submit bids. Bidders with reasonable prices may not be invited if the public official in charge does not have sufficient overview of the market or if she intentionally excludes reasonable bids from the process on account of extralegal cooperation with other bidders. Public officials have the greatest discretionary power in the *single tender action,* for which they merely have to document their informal request for bids. As a rule, there are control regulations that set a maximum limit on the value of contracts for which a single bid or restricted tender is permitted.

An effective tender requires a precise description of products and services. Without adequate precision, it is not possible to compare bids.[2] Clients and bidders can avoid contacting each other during the tendering process (an activity vulnerable to misuse) only if services and products are described in a sufficiently detailed manner.

A contract is awarded to a bidder on the basis of the so-called best bidder principle, and not on the basis of the lowest bidder principle. Because the aspect of quality has to be considered in awarding contracts, it would be inappropriate to automatically grant a contract to the lowest bidder. Consequently, even in a properly executed tendering process, the office responsible for granting contracts inevitably has more or less restricted discretionary powers in evaluating quality and selecting the best bidder.

One can deduce from the description above that the procurement process provides many opportunities for corruption: If a tendering process is restricted or if interested parties have to pass a prequalification round to become bidders, public officials could demand bribe money in exchange for spots on the bidder list. Officials could also inform one bidder about the prices of competing bids and then allow that one bidder to submit a backdated, revised bid, thus appearing to be the "best bidder." In both cases, public officials have an extralegal advantage in the form of income from bribe payments.

In order to secure a kickback, tendering has to be steered in such a way that the contractor who will later agree to overpricing and a corresponding return payment appears to be the best bidder. There are a number of manipulation schemes for reaching this goal: (1) the competing bidders in a closed tender are manipulatively selected; (2) obstacles are set for competing bidders in an open bidding process (the call for bids is not published in widely read publications or the publicized deadline for submitting bids is very short while the preselected contract winner is informed in advance); or (3) requirements are formulated in such a way that only one or a few bidders can meet them.[3] If more reasonable bidders cannot be fended off by one of these schemes, there is always the possibility of simply declaring the desired contract winner the best bidder on the grounds of completely arbitrary criteria.

The process may be tied to a tender collusion among all bidders. In this kind of arrangement, competing bidders do not even want to win a contract; rather, they are familiar with the bid by the preselected contract winner and intentionally submit offers priced above it. In another scenario, they may purposely design their offers so that the process favors the predetermined "winner," for example, by setting extremely long delivery dates. Participation in such fictitious procurement processes is, indeed, attractive to an "inferior" bidder: Either there is a system of rotating contract winners among the companies involved in tender collusion—an "inferior" bidder becomes the predetermined winner in another bidding process and profits with everyone from the exclusion of "organized competition," which is what bidding should actually guarantee. Or an "inferior" bidder receives payment from the predetermined winner—payment that, in the end, also has to be covered by deviated public funds.

The group of World Bank employees in Indonesia who tried to quantify the extent of embezzlement in aid projects is convinced that all bidders for contracts from public offices have to pay a sum of less than 1 percent of the total project value in order to pass the prequalification procedure and that collusion occurs frequently in procurement processes. The "winner" in turn pays 1–2 percent of the total project volume to each "inferior" bidder.[4] In awarding some research contracts through public offices, which I gained insight into during my time as a project leader in Indonesia, officials in charge very simply passed the problem of acquiring more expensive competing bids on to the predetermined contract winner. Considering the number of university and nonuniversity institutes and consulting firms whose directors knew each other personally and helped each other along, that method worked for everyone. To simplify administrative work, they even exchanged letterheads.

The Limited Effect of Administrative Controls

Processes for formally securing misappropriation also occur where misappropriation is common practice, where control mechanisms either do not exist, or where supervising bodies are actually involved in distributing misappropriated gains. Those processes not only serve to secure embezzlement schemes when external donors attempt to implement budget stipulations from donor countries, but also originate from participating officials weighing the risks of control mechanisms within recipient countries. They do not know whether control procedures will be changed in the future. There is no permanence to the real tolerance of misappropriation. It can be reversed at any time without violating the nonretroactivity principle; officials responsible for controlling corruption might simply cease ignoring laws that had always been valid. Investigation of past administrative activities was used to gather information for an anticorruption campaign in Southeast and East Asian countries.[5] Public officials are even subject to the risk of controls in cases in which governments have no intention of restricting corruption. Investigation into past activities can serve as a pretext for dismissing otherwise permanent staff, or an investigation can be carried out with the goal of removing certain officials from office so that those in charge have room to hire new, no less corrupt staff members who will be indebted to them. The danger of retroactive investigation alone will compel public officials who are aware of the risks to cover up embezzlement schemes in such a way that later, their violation of official rules can either not be proven at all or only with great difficulty.

Wherever elaborate procedures are common for falsifying receipts and manipulating procurement processes to secure misappropriation, administrative control mechanisms fall short of their goal. Foreign donors do not have the authority backed by domestic law to effectively check submitted receipts. They do not have the traditional law enforcement powers usually available to national authorities, "such as subpoena power or the ability to otherwise compel the production of documents or witness testimony or to conduct searches or electronic surveillance."[6] For example, foreign donors cannot check whether a supplier's records bear an entry that corresponds to an issued receipt or whether the income for which a receipt has been issued is included in tax forms. As a result, foreign sponsors have no opportunity to use bookkeeping oversight to pick up on clues pointing to a kickback arrangement. Administrative control mechanisms on the donor's part are inevitably limited under such conditions. Therefore, when sponsors draw attention to the special control processes used in disbursing their funds, they usually do so just to soothe themselves. As soon as external project funds are put into the hands of government officials in the recipient country, the same practices apply as with the disbursement of other government funds. One can only assume there might be a difference if the external financer is able to push through special controls. But in order to do so, she has to intervene personally in administrative procedures because the documents she would need to support control mechanisms are produced by officials who collaborate to cover up embezzlement schemes.

That does not mean that administrative rules are completely useless. They do oblige project partners to state how project funds were spent and to document procurement processes for large-scale contracts. However, it is impossible, on the basis of administrative control regulations alone, to draw conclusions as to whether a project is free of misappropriation. More far-reaching instruments of corruption control are necessary to draw such conclusions. Independent inquiries by foreign donors into market prices or the investment costs of comparable projects restrict the playing field for kickback arrangements. Infrastructure and construction projects may suffer from poor quality and reduced lifespan of facilities due to large-scale misappropriation schemes, unless those responsible for misappropriation had anticipated extralegal costs in the budget-planning phase. Botched-up jobs that result from misappropriation are sometimes overlooked until well after completion of a project. Examining a project after completion can also provide information regarding misappropriation during the execution phase, or it can reveal evidence proving that a project was carried out according to specifications. In evaluating the mechanisms of corruption control within Caritas Bangladesh, I found it most convincing that the cyclone shelters built years ago had withstood heavy cyclones and spring tides without any signs of damage. That can be the case only when construction supervision is not circumvented via corruption.[7]

Administrative control regulations are related to procedures. They are used to check whether funds have been allocated according to budget and whether procedures fixed with the aim of controlling misuse have been adhered to. The external sponsor of development projects very often lacks evidence when she sees reason to doubt the validity of receipts submitted to her. As mentioned earlier, she is not authorized to carry out an effective check; the local environment may also not even permit an effective check. If controls for aid projects are more strongly tied to effectiveness, external sponsors can compensate for the lack of evidence that receipts are fraudulent by checking the work done against the specifications for that work.

Leaving the Job to the External Sponsor

Corruption control may be more thorough when project implementation remains in the hands of the external sponsor and foreign staff members manage the procurement process and award contracts themselves. Foreign staff members receive salaries commensurate with or higher than the usual salaries in the donor country. If they misbehave, they run the risk of losing their attractive jobs and, due to the exchange of information among development organizations, of never finding another job in their field. In addition, they are subject to criminal sanctions in their home countries. Various moral or cultural factors aside, the risk calculation of a foreign staff member leads to different behavior from the risk calculation of a public official in a developing country who belongs to a group in which receiving illegal side income is both tolerated and the order of the day. Foreign aid sponsors can carry out corruption control simply by leaving project implementation in the hands of foreign staff, thus maintaining a firewall between the project and administrative structures in the recipient country. This kind of isolated approach is often preferred in the field of technical cooperation. Expatriate staff members working in programs of technical cooperation make allocation decisions themselves or in cooperation with their headquarters. This isolated approach may appear advantageous for corruption control and may even be justifiable in some areas of technical cooperation. However, it is not a good solution. It negates the responsibility of recipient countries and, with it, an important precondition for successful development rightfully defined by aid policy debate about the failure of many projects.[8] The isolated approach replaces the responsibility of recipient countries with external intervention. It is certainly not good in the long term because it does not help to establish more efficient administrative structures in recipient countries. It can even serve to diminish external pressure to reform public administration.[9] And—regardless of what one thinks of it—using external staff on projects runs up against capacity barriers; it cannot be used, in particular, in large-scale financial aid projects. External leaders of such large projects cannot avoid delegating mid- and low-level management tasks to local officials. If local officials, in turn, take advantage of the common practice of deviating funds, cooperating with third parties to secure illegal schemes, as is done in the government sector of the respective recipient country, then controlling corruption will be at best difficult in an environment without control structures. It is therefore obvious that effective corruption control in aid cooperation cannot be achieved through isolated project implementation. Effective corruption control requires progress toward more transparency in the government sector of recipient countries. I will address this issue in greater detail in Chapter 12.

Notes

1. On the following, see Aicher (1981); Marschdorf (1999), pp. 437ff; Wiehen (1999, 2001).

2. Both a constructive and a functional description of services are possible. Difficulties in describing planning services in a planning phase with few concrete terms can necessitate a single tender action.

3. Aguilar, Gill, and Pino (2000), pp. 4–5.

4. World Bank Resident Staff, Indonesia (1998).

5. See case studies by Klitgaard (1988), in particular pp. 53–54, 82ff.

6. See Thornburgh (2004), p. 3, on the limitations the World Bank faces in addressing fraud and corruption. Of course, the argument is valid for all foreign donors.

7. See Cremer (1996), p. 171.

8. Bastøe and Masst (2001), pp. 71–72.

9. See, for example, the discussion of "enclaving" within the World Bank. See World Bank (1997a), p. 54.

8

The Role of Nongovernmental Organizations

CORRUPTION IN DEVELOPING COUNTRIES IS CONSIDERED, AT first glance, a problem of the public sector. Civil servants have discretionary powers from which opportunities for bribery arise, and they administer the public budget, which provides them with possibilities for misappropriation. Partly because of a desire to counter the misuse of funds, the spectrum of partners within development work has diversified since the 1970s.[1] Even government bodies that used to work exclusively on a state-to-state basis are now trying to expand their tools of providing aid to include nongovernmental organizations. NGOs in donor countries have become recipients of public funding and sponsors of local NGOs in developing countries, thus making them sponsors of bodies outside the public sector.

Corruption as an internal problem in implementing project plans is, however, not limited to the public sector. Managers and staff of nongovernmental organizations hold positions comparable to those of public officials, positions they can misuse to fulfill private purposes. The mechanisms for deviating funds within nongovernmental organizations are not essentially different from the mechanisms found in public organizations. For example, misappropriation schemes are secured through kickback agreements in the private and nonprofit sectors as well. NGOs in developing countries long enjoyed a comparatively good reputation. Of course, that good reputation had its roots in a time when aid flowed primarily from government to government. Thus, the founding of an NGO did not furnish access to divertible funds. But once donors decided to allocate funds to nongovernmental organizations as a reaction to inefficiency within the state sector, those circumstances changed. Nowadays, even smaller developing countries have numerous NGOs that compete for access to aid funds.[2]

Within this rapid growth period, two developments have overlapped. First, a reorientation of aid policy toward greater consideration of nongovernmental organizations created the initial financial foundation needed for growth in the first place. Second, the expansion of school systems within many developing countries has led to increasing numbers of secondary school and university graduates. Those graduates cannot all find jobs in the government sector, as was the case in the past, because the expansion of public services cannot, for fiscal reasons, keep up with the expansion in education. The private sector can only partially absorb job-seeking graduates. Following university, many graduates have great difficulty finding a job commensurate with their education. As a result, the job-seeking phase following graduation is often very long.[3] Founding an NGO with the hope of receiving foreign aid creates a possibility for securing a job commensurate with one's education. Thus NGOs initially serve the purpose of employing their founders, a purpose that is not intrinsically illegitimate.[4] NGOs constitute, one could say, the informal sector for university graduates.

Moreover, the state sector and the NGO sector do not form completely separate worlds. As long as the registration of an NGO or the implementation of projects requires state approval, government bodies can influence who gains access to aid funds by means of successfully founding an NGO. Family members of administration officials also establish NGOs. They have privileged access to information regarding the availability of funds for nongovernmental development activities, thus making it worthwhile for them to start up an NGO. Hence, the formal nongovernmental character of an institution is no guarantee that development funds will not be misused.

Risks Specific to Nongovernmental Organizations

Special kinds of risks arise from the informal character of NGOs and the peculiarities of sponsorship by foreign, usually nonstate, donors. Despite the many gaps in state control regulations, there are at least fixed procedures for recording receipts and expenditures and for bidding out contracts. As discussed earlier, these procedures are circumvented in a variety of creative ways, but they do restrict misappropriation to a certain extent because of the risk factor involved for public officials. Nongovernmental organizations do not necessarily have control mechanisms. It is possible that the founders or managers of an NGO will decide for themselves to install financial controlling regulations, that state laws and ordinances will demand proof of control and the state actually enforces its laws, or that foreign donors will require clear agreements on financial management as a condition of their willingness to send money. But, often, none of the above conditions is fulfilled.

Consequently, many nongovernmental organizations do not have even the most rudimentary financial controlling systems. This is especially true of many smaller organizations that enjoy popularity based on the ideology of "small is beautiful." Without financial controls, the founders' main motive of self-employment can easily turn into self-enrichment. Without at least rudimentary structures of financial management, it is not possible to check whether all foreign funds have been properly booked as income for the organization. Financial reports sent to foreign donors are often artificially compiled if there are no mechanisms for checking them against bookkeeping records. Because of the lack of a consolidated financial report, there is no great risk involved in having the same project sponsored twice by two foreign partners, especially if the sponsors are located in different countries and have no contact with each other.

Without a transparent, rigorous payroll system, wages may be increased on a whim. Daily stipends for project trips are particularly vulnerable. Managers may accumulate various jobs: They are, at the same time, directors of their respective organizations and managers of diverse projects for which they receive separate payment. Note that a manager's tasks are often reduced to written correspondence with the foreign donor, while field workers do the real project work. Simultaneously, managers are remunerated for their work as resource persons for other NGOs, sometimes in reciprocal business arrangements.

In the invoice she receives, the foreign sponsor sees only one element of the accumulated compensation package, leaving her under the illusion that her partner organization aims to serve the "poorest of the poor," as evident in the apparently modest manager's income. Accumulated compensation from various jobs is not illegitimate per se, and in countries where poorly paid government employees live off income from second and third jobs, it is not unusual. However, without control and transparency, accumulated compensation schemes become a system for filling one's own pockets. Forms of nontransparent money transfer include the allocation of loans to NGO staff members without any controls over repayment and recompense for private expenses (e.g., gasoline or telephone fees) from project money.

Foreign sponsors bear a substantial part of the responsibility when such practices develop within their nongovernmental partner organizations. In the early years of foreign sponsorship, it was considered an expression of mistrust and incompatible with the spirit of partnership to require straightforward agreements on financial controls, yet such agreements are essential to clarify the relationship between donors and their partners. Experience with NGOs has so far clearly shown that misuse of funds is not a phenomenon peculiar to the state sector alone. Today there is less emotional resistance on the part of donors to requiring professional financial management. Of course, representatives of NGOs in developing countries still occasionally accuse sponsors of unjust interventionism or colonial paternalism whenever rules are enforced to attain transparency.

Donors are also at fault when they link their own tolerance of nontransparency to rhetoric stipulating that NGO staff members live like their target groups, namely like the "poorest of the poor." Staff members in recipient countries who work directly with foreign donors have degrees from universities and speak universal languages suitable for global communication (e.g., English, French, or Spanish). After all, those are prerequisites for their ability to communicate with foreign donors who typically do not speak the local language. Staff members are of the middle class and expect wages to support a lifestyle on a par with the middle class of their home country. They want to send their children to schools representative of their class; in many developing countries that means costly private schools. "Poorest of the poor" rhetoric is useless; it only serves as an excuse for NGOs and donors to neglect negotiating openly about wages commensurate with staff qualifications and necessary administrative costs. Managers obtain a middle-class salary by accumulating compensation as described above. Without transparency, some may receive inappropriately large compensation packages.

Furthermore, foreign sponsors contribute to the kinds of practices described above whenever they support recipient organizations on a selective, irregular basis rather than committing themselves to long-term cooperation. Without a long-term commitment, foreign donors cannot look closely into the structures of their partner organizations. Many years of cooperation are required for foreign donors to help partners become more professional in managing their projects and finances. Another advantage to long-term cooperation is the greater chance of actually enforcing the contract between a foreign donor and its partner, as the misuse of funds puts long-term relationships on the line. Foreign sponsors also contribute to less-than-transparent working methods when their requirements do not take the institutional interests of their partner organization into consideration. Partners are then forced to resort to crooked methods in order to adhere to their own institutional interests. This aspect of the relationship between foreign donors and domestic NGOs will be discussed separately in Chapter 10.

The Advantage of Choice

Although corruption is not unheard of within the NGO sector, development work with NGOs, in comparison to work done exclusively between government bodies, does have a central advantage with regard to controlling misuse. NGOs, unlike state bodies, are partners for development work who do not hold a monopoly over a region or a sector. A sponsor who works exclusively with state-run offices has few alternatives when confronted with practices of misuse and when his governmental partner is reluctant to abandon these practices. She can decide to discontinue cooperation with her government partner, but that generally means she would have to stop working in that particular sector and region. Cooperation with another government body would not be possible because each level of government has fixed areas of responsibility within the region and the sector. The sponsor may decide to continue working with the state partner who has proven to be dubious. As a result of monopolies held by state partners, the threshold for cutting off a partnership is much higher. With a variety of NGOs at hand, however, a foreign sponsor has choices. Competition for donations arises among NGOs active in developing countries. Faced with proof of misuse or nontransparent project implementation, foreign donors can take the logical steps, all the way to ending cooperation, without having to completely cease their work in their particular sector or region.

Consequently, foreign sponsors bear great responsibility for making decisions that contribute to the establishment of efficient and transparent working systems in NGOs. In defining their requirements for sponsorship, including requirements for financial management, foreign donors can influence competition among independent aid organizations.

Notes

1. Other reasons are the assumed or real closer ties between NGOs and target groups, and the ability to bypass bureaucracy in the state sector. Camerer (2001), p. 190, reports that the direct targeting of NGOs in South Africa allowed donors to circumvent complicated state tendering procedures. Government departments also formed alliances with NGOs to avoid such regulations.

2. There are no comprehensive statistics on NGOs. The available data leave no doubt that their number has increased many times over since the beginning of the 1980s. See Sklias (1999), pp. 28ff, 85ff.

3. See Cremer (1995), pp. 101ff, 175ff, for an example from Indonesia.

4. See the excellent case study by Wegner (1994) for an example of an NGO that was born principally of the employment motives of its founders.

9

Barriers to Information in Development Work

TO WHAT EXTENT ARE STAFF MEMBERS OF SPONSORING organizations willing and able to detect facts that hint at misappropriation in projects they support? Are there barriers to the flow of information in cases in which certain knowledge would force one to take appropriate steps, steps that might contradict the institutional interests of the organization or result in negative consequences for individuals who reveal the facts?[1] Foreign donors, on the one hand, and the staff of an organization in a recipient country, on the other, do not share equal access to relevant information anyway. Available evidence that hints at misappropriation or other forms of corruption can only be considered relevant after a thorough investigation and careful evaluation. If a foreign donor provides financial support only, then it is limited to checking financial reports and reports by officials, appraisers, and evaluators. If a foreign donor deploys its own staff to the project location, an additional channel of information opens.

It only makes sense to detect evidence pointing to corruption if the sponsoring organization is willing to take the next logical step based on that evidence. The sponsor could engage in intense talks with the project partner, change project design, or, in the worst-case scenario, cut off sponsorship. When there are overriding political or institutional reasons for continuing sponsorship under all circumstances, staff members of the sponsoring organization will either avoid picking up on corruption-related evidence or they will not invest much energy into looking for such evidence. The documentation of large-scale misappropriation merely creates difficulties in having to justify a program that cannot be stopped.[2] The end of the

Cold War signaled the loss of the most important overriding interest in carrying on aid projects despite corruption. In turn, that loss set the stage for ridding corruption of its taboos.

What Foreign Aid Workers Actually Perceive

Foreign aid workers can be an essential source of information about corruption in project implementation. Whether this source of information is actually used by deploying organizations or by donors to sanction misappropriation depends on whether foreign aid workers take advantage of their opportunities to gather information and whether information flows to decisionmakers.

Along those lines, the willingness of foreign aid workers to notice corruption is of primary importance. The perception of misuse can be blocked in a foreign worker's own project if such facts lead to cognitive dissonance. In accordance with cognitive consistency theories of social psychology, people try to avoid contradictions in their cognitions—opinions, convictions, values—about themselves and certain aspects of their surroundings. People try to avoid such contradictions because they find inconsistency between two cognitions unreasonable or unpleasant.[3] An individual tends either to avoid situations that increase cognitive dissonance or to restructure his cognitions in a way that either provides for consistency or at least reduces dissonance. Possibilities for restructuring include the selective acquisition of information and varying interpretations of available information.

The perception of misuse-related facts in one's own project work surely produces cognitive dissonance in a foreign aid worker who has taken up his post with the intention of helping people. He can avoid or reduce those cognitive dissonances by simply turning a blind eye to facts pointing to misuse or by interpreting such facts to make them look like marginal exceptions. As social psychological experiments have shown, the more indistinctly an object presents itself, the easier it is to interpret it in a variety of ways. Facts pointing to misuse are often presented as unclear objects because, as mentioned earlier, the people involved adhere to certain security procedures in order to minimize their risk. In general, actors will shield information from foreign aid workers because they represent potential informants for the body that might cut off funding.

Corrupt contracts are often negotiated in scrambled messages, which require ample intercultural competence to interpret, a competence a foreign aid worker may not possess. Indirect forms of communication are, on the one hand, a cultural characteristic in many countries; on the other hand, they also serve to minimize risk. Using scrambled messages, a potential partner in a corrupt contract can allude to his willingness to participate without facing criminal risk from the start.

The more persistently evidence of misuse occurs in a foreign worker's project and the longer he has the opportunity to become acquainted with local forms of communication, the more difficult it is for him to dismiss or marginalize information pointing to misuse. Even if an individual feels the need to avoid cognitive dissonance and even if the acquisition of information is hindered by blurred signals in corrupt contract negotiations, foreign aid workers can still be used as a source of information on evidence of corruption. It seems to me, at any rate, that experienced project leaders are more often disillusioned, or are even hardened cynics, rather than naive believers in good.

What Foreign Aid Workers Want to Tell Their Head Office

Foreign aid workers frequently have a dual function in technical cooperation projects: They serve as consultants to project partners and, at the same time, are responsible for the accuracy of the facts and accounts in their projects. Even when a representative of the partner organization in the recipient country bears the title "project leader," it is often the foreign staff member from the dispatching organization who is really in charge.[4] He is answerable for the correct implementation of a project. News of misuse-related facts at a certain point during project implementation could cast a shadow on his earlier confirmation that a project is running properly. Such news could also damage the image of a foreign staff member if he took part in the conceptual phase of project planning and selected the partner organization. The decisive factor in these cases is how the dispatching organization deals with such information. If it is used as evidence against a foreign staff member to show he has failed to do a good job, then the flow of information will inevitably be blocked. Because corruption has been a taboo within dispatching organizations and often foreign staff members are not trained to control misuse, foreign staff must often fear that information hinting at misappropriation might reflect badly upon themselves.[5]

Even if information about misuse did not damage the reputation of a foreign staff member, he would still have reasons to be careful about passing on such information. He cannot anticipate all possible consequences. His dispatching organization might impose conditions for further project work that he fears he will not be able to fulfill, or the donor organization may decide to react more drastically and stop the project or any planned extension of it. If his contract is for that project only and the project is canceled, he may lose his job.

What the Head Office Wants to Know

Barriers to information can also arise from the interests of a dispatching organization or the people who work there. When a foreign staff member shares misuse-related information with his contact in the head office, it does not necessarily mean that those who could decide what steps to take are actually informed. Desk officers in the headquarters of dispatching organizations might also harbor fears that their own project-related decisions will be second-guessed.

Special risks arise for the dispatching organization when a project has been funded with public money. That is always the case in state-to-state development aid, but projects by nongovernmental organizations also are financed by public funds. A recipient of public funding is responsible for ensuring that those funds are used for the purpose stipulated in approval papers. However, recipients have only a limited degree of control over the conditions of project implementation. Misuse of project funds by a partner organization or its local personnel is, by definition, a breach of approval conditions. If that misuse is put on record, funding recipients may be confronted with demands for repayment by either the donor or the auditing office. Such situations can threaten the existence of smaller organizations that are primarily funded by public means. It is all too obvious that such dangers create blockades to the perception and processing of information pointing to corruption.

This should not be taken as a plea to simply release recipients of public funds from their responsibility for the proper implementation of projects. However, barriers to information can only be overcome if demands for repayment are dealt with in a sensible manner. Controlling bodies should acknowledge that project implementation in countries where corruption is an everyday phenomenon will inevitably entail certain risks and that there may be underlying reasons for misuse that recipients cannot control. There is anecdotal evidence indicating that some of the governments funding NGO aid projects are beginning to take that into consideration. Some desk officers of aid organizations report that in recent years they have actually dared to speak with their government donors about the risks of corruption in the projects they are funding. I personally know a few examples in which government donors refrained from demanding to recover their funds after a recipient aid organization had reported cases of embezzlement in a government-funded project. The government funding agency acknowledged that the corruption was not the result of culpable or neglectful behavior inside the aid organization that had channeled the funds to its partner organization abroad. In one particular case, the hard and fast way the recipient aid organization handled the fraud case and documented it transparently was considered exemplary. These cases give us reason to hope that the "it is better not to know" attitude is gradually retreating, which is a precondition for reducing barriers to information.

The existence of such barriers, both between a foreign staff member and his dispatching organization and within dispatching organizations, does not necessarily imply that obvious and clearly documented misuse-related evidence is hidden from higher authorities. By concealing information, foreign staff and desk officers in the dispatching office would run the risk of neglecting their duties, and if the information became known through another source, they would be subject to reproach. Instead, when foreign staff members or desk officers in the head office have to fear that their perception of certain clues might result in undesirable consequences for themselves or their organization, they simply will not actively seek out those clues.

To what extent it might be rational to hide misuse-related information depends on the extent of independent sources of information available to the authority from whom information is concealed. It becomes more difficult to detect misuse with increasing distance from the level of project implementation. As described earlier, misappropriation is secured through certain procedures for producing receipts or other bogus forms of proof. If such procedures are followed carefully, very detailed knowledge is required to gain insight into individual cases, and distant authorities usually do not have that detailed knowledge. Strong effectiveness-oriented analysis of project results provides offshore authorities with greater chances of acquiring independent information. Large-scale misappropriation always leads to grave differences between the plan and its implementation, provided that an organization can prevent misappropriation schemes from inflating the budget. When external donors are able to establish independently that budgetary differences are due to misappropriation, then information barriers become ominous to all those involved in the scheme. They must create plausible explanations for the discrepancies between the plan and its implementation, if they want to keep their knowledge of the misuse of project funds to themselves.

Notes

1. See, on the following, Cremer (1998a), pp. 15ff; Cremer (2004). On barriers to information in the appraisal of development projects, see Wolff (2001).
2. On obstacles to detecting major facts constituting corruption in a Cold War–era project, see the analysis of the US Food Aid Program in Zaire, Gould (1979), p. 265.
3. Bierbrauer (1979). This refers back to the theory of cognitive dissonance by L. Festinger (1957, 1978).
4. For a comparison between partnership rhetoric and reality, see Braun (1988), pp. 356ff.
5. Barriers to information prevail in the private sector too. Singh (1999), p. 409, refers to a survey on internal control in US companies: "While only 11% of CEOs and 19% of CFOs say that employees are taking some risk in reporting bad news, 36% of middle managers and 48% of non-management employees believe they take some risk in reporting bad news in their companies."

10

The Pressure to Spend "Development Dollars"

WORD HAS FOUND ITS WAY INTO OFFICIAL ANNOUNCEMENTS that pressure to disburse funds is prevalent in the field of development cooperation.[1] In other words, development aid organizations are under pressure to allocate funds even when they harbor doubts about whether those funds can be usefully absorbed. Disbursement pressure is a subject of importance in the context at hand because it constitutes one of the structural factors that make it difficult to check corruption and to create risks for misuse. Another structural factor with the same impact is an overly restrictive set of guidelines that hampers successful project implementation and provokes people in charge to bend the rules. In addition, the demonization of administrative costs, especially in organizations funded by private donations, can lead to a situation in which the personnel necessary to properly accompany and supervise projects can no longer be guaranteed.

Structural Forces Within Aid Organizations

Disbursement pressures give the impression that there is money in abundance in the area of development aid. Of course, that is not true in relationship to the sum of problems that need to be solved in developing countries. Neither does it apply to all projects for which there are ample conditions for implementation and which deserve foreign support. However, there can be an overabundance of funding with regard to individual countries, regions, or operational sectors.[2] Disbursement pressures can arise when funding is earmarked to serve a certain purpose. For example, funds may be earmarked for use in the poorest of developing countries or for projects that fight poverty, improve education, or restore the environment. The stipulations resulting from such decisions are legally binding; legislative bodies and the public will measure the efficiency of development aid against quantitative adherence to those stipulations.[3]

Disbursement pressures can arise from expenditure deadlines set forth by regulations such as year-end closings for public budgets. They can also result from the objectives and tactical considerations of development aid organizations. Earmarked funds and expenditure deadlines prevent money from flowing to other regions, to other sectors, or at a later point in time (if areas designated to receive aid do not or do not yet meet the requirements for worthwhile project work).

Disbursement pressures are also present whenever the central office of an aid organization finances its administrative expenses from project administration fees. A certain percentage of project funds is used to cover personnel and other costs. If high standards are applied in preliminary project inspections, the total volume of money spent and, with it, administration fees, may decrease. This, in turn, might jeopardize jobs in the central office. In the event that project funding is cut off after corrupt practices have been revealed, there will inevitably be negative consequences for administrative income in the sponsoring organization. Administration fees are generally based on actual amounts spent and not on planned numbers.

Pressure to disburse funds can also be rooted in the tactical considerations of the recipient organization with regard to its public donor organization. If the volume of funds spent by a recipient decreases over a certain period of time, the future availability of funds might be based on lower forecast estimates. Any decision by the recipient to cut off funding to a local partner includes an admission to the donor organization that estimates made in the project application were incorrect and, if corruption plays a role, that the recipient organization made mistakes in selecting local project partners. The extent to which such tactical considerations play a role is determined by how project delays or cancellations are interpreted. If people in charge of the donor organization believe that the smooth and uninterrupted implementation of a project plan provides decisive proof of efficiency in a recipient organization, then they contribute to barriers in information flow and to disbursement pressures.

Disbursement pressures can also occur within organizations or projects financed by private donations. Private donors determine the purpose for which their donations shall be spent. Deadlines for expenditure result from stipulations set forth by tax authorities and from tactical considerations by the organizations involved. Since the mid-1990s, the tax offices in Germany have become more restrictive in defining what they accept as the "timely" utilization of funds. German tax offices have the right to impose deadlines on nonprofit organizations for expending tax-deductible donations. An organization can lose its nonprofit status if it does not use these funds in a timely manner. Increasingly restrictive financial policies can increase the pressure on organizations to expend donations earlier than necessary or to subject donations to very narrowly defined purposes. Disbursement pressures can result from these circumstances.[4]

However, of far greater importance is the disbursement pressure that results from tactics employed by organizations to enhance their ability to attract private donations. This is a virulent problem for nonstate disaster relief, which is largely financed by donations.[5] Private donations are acquired primarily when disasters are current and thus extensively covered by the media. At such times, organizations competing for donations have to prove their competence through effective publicity. In doing so, they often harm longer-term rehabilitation projects that receive far less or no attention from the media, rendering them barely significant in the field of fund-raising. Particularly in the event of a large-scale disaster, numerous NGOs compete for short-term placement in the media—a form of competition that is also counterproductive to any attempts at controlling misuse during project implementation.

The Effects of Disbursement Pressure

What effect does disbursement pressure have on the ability of aid organizations to control misuse of their funds? It has implications both for preventing corruption and for reacting to it. It is plausible to imagine that decisionmakers experiencing disbursement pressure tend to be less careful in preselecting projects than they would be without such pressure. If the preselection process shows that structures for implementing a particular project are insufficient, then that knowledge interferes with the goal of expending funds according to deadlines and to budgets drawn up by region or sector. The preselection phase also involves aspects that are relevant to preventing corruption, such as determining the seriousness of a local partner, putting together careful descriptions of project goals and expected results (prerequisites for result-oriented checks), and inspecting budget estimates for any potential for the deviation of funds. So much for the preventative aspect.

Disbursement pressure also affects an aid organization's ability to react to evidence of misuse while a project is running. Any decision to end project funding or to refuse extension of a project also conflicts with disbursement stipulations. Organizations that receive public funding are faced with a particular problem. If they happen upon evidence related to misuse and thus demand that a local partner or local contractor fulfill contract requirements, refusing or delaying payment to underline their demand, they could run into conflicts with budgetary approval periods. Such organizations run the risk of having to return their funding. Furthermore, the recipient organization is usually obliged to pay interest to its donor if it cannot meet deadlines. This kind of pressure to expend weakens negotiating leverage with local partners and contractors. One should not forget that local partners and contractors are at least roughly aware of the practices of public project financing. They might even know very well that their foreign partner or client is on tenterhooks because any delay of payment can be very expensive. Of course, disbursement pressures do not remain hidden from partners in developing countries. Pressures to expend reduce the incentive for local partners to check misuse within their own organizations because misuse does not necessarily harm a program's target group. Instead, it is charged to the budgets of donor organizations under disbursement pressure. Ethical hurdles to practices of misuse may be lower if the local staff members of a partner organization sense that more than enough funding is available, at least in relation to the locally practicable possibilities for providing aid.

Excessive Demands on Local Partners

Disbursement pressures can lead to excessive demands on partners in developing countries. Honest, experienced, and competent partner organizations constitute a bottleneck in international cooperation. When various foreign sponsors that concentrate on the same region and the same field of work are subject to disbursement pressures, a situation can arise in which sponsors compete for the few competent local partner organizations at hand. Such situations come about in particular during disasters receiving international attention and during ensuing periods of reconstruction. For helping victims of those disasters under intensive media attention, relief organizations obtain high levels of revenue from private donations, and at the same time government bodies are equally interested in providing funds in an atmosphere of highly effective publicity. Because public interest quickly wanes, sponsors of disaster relief are vehemently interested in making their work visible during the acute phase of a disaster. Pressure to disburse may result. Decisions made by public donors heighten disbursement pressures: They are more willing to give funds during highly publicized disasters than during disasters hidden in the shadows. In doing so, they often foster a cyclical pattern of sponsorship policy that coincides with revenues from private donations.[6] Pressure to expend funds can also harm those partners in disaster relief that had shown integrity and been successful in checking internal misuse up to the start of an acute disaster with great media attention. Under the conditions of disbursement pressure, competent local sponsors in particular face pressure to expand their programs to an extent that overtaxes their own structures. Of course, it is also difficult for trustworthy organizations to restrict themselves to a reasonable scale of activity when foreign funding is more easily had during an acute phase. A rapid expansion of programs induced by the offer of foreign funds requires expanding administrative structures, hiring additional personnel whose reliability may be questionable, or starting up activities in regions where local partners have neither experience nor contacts. All these factors make it difficult for partners to control misuse within their organizations. Disbursement pressures thus hold the danger of overtaxing local organizations and, in the worst-case scenario, destroying their integrity.[7]

Overly Restrictive Guidelines and Rule Bending

Practices suited to formally securing misappropriation are also used in development cooperation projects to make restrictive guidelines more "flexible," and by no means exclusively by local project partners, but also by foreign staff members in charge of projects on location. Restrictive guidelines may include expenditure deadlines that cannot be met due to circumstances that delay the progress of a project. If it is not possible to spend all project funding in accordance with deadlines, then, under the strict conditions of year-end budgeting, any funding left has to be paid back and considered a loss for the project. In a country where the service of a supplier includes issuing receipts whenever the customer pleases, it may be possible to rescue lost funds by postdating documents.

Another guideline that may be considered restrictive is the stipulation that funds be used only for specific target groups; the project can be jeopardized when the target group is too narrowly defined. For instance, in refugee relief, if funds are earmarked for exclusive use in aiding a refugee target group, thus excluding the surrounding population that often has similar needs, adverse feelings toward refugee camps might arise or be amplified and ultimately hinder the integration of refugees. Project leaders interested in lessening the tension between refugees and their surrounding population will open program services (e.g., a health care station) to the neighbors of refugee camps. If they are actually not allowed to do so because of senseless rules laid down by their dispatching organization or by donors, those project leaders will be tempted to solve the problem by disguising target group information in their project reports.

Budgets that do not allow local partners to pay employees at a level commensurate with their qualifications can also be mentioned here. Inadequate pay may lead to practices in NGOs similar to those in state-run organizations. If it is easy under project circumstances to make a kickback arrangement with a supplier, then kickback profits can be used to increase wages in a manner not visible to the donor organization, and qualified employees can be kept on staff.

The examples given above do not constitute corruption, in the sense of abuse of discretionary powers, if the person in charge does not fill his private coffers. People in charge use such methods with the sole intention of reaching or more effectively fulfilling project goals. It is better for the fulfillment of project goals to postdate receipts than to try to meet year-end deadlines in a "December rush." Having said all that, these "rule-bending" methods are disadvantageous from the viewpoint of corruption control. They require procedures to secure success that are identical or similar to procedures used to disguise misappropriation. If the attainment of project goals depends on such methods, the people in charge cannot possibly be interested in transparency in project organization, even if they do not strive for unjust personal advantage.

Discrepancies between receipts and reports on the one hand and reality on the other are often noticed by local project staff, who cannot discern whether certain methods are being used to bend the rules of project implementation or whether their bosses are using those methods to fill their own pockets. Staff members notice, for example, that sales receipts show prices clearly much higher than the going market rates, and they assume a kickback arrangement. Unlike external donors, staff members cannot be kept in the dark because they are aware of local conditions. However, they cannot figure out what happens to profits from kickback arrangements. A situation like that can diminish an employee's inhibitions regarding misuse of project money. It is natural to assume that such methods serve personal goals in an environment where corruption is an ordinary phenomenon. If foreign sponsors insist on transparency—and they should for reasons of corruption control—they are responsible for providing sponsorship guidelines that allow for the fulfillment of project goals without rule bending.

Restrictive guidelines can also hamper local partners in openly pursuing their legitimate institutional interests. This is a particularly virulent problem in the sponsorship of nongovernmental organizations that depend, for better or for worse, on external financing for their existence.[8] Their fundamental problem is committing to long-term obligations, such as paying their core group of employees and maintaining their infrastructure, in the face of unstable and discontinued external financial sources. Because NGOs in donating countries depend on somewhat short-term decisionmaking by public donors or on unpredictable fluctuation on the fund-raising market, they are often unable to make long-term, binding commitments. Financial reserves that accrue interest then used to cover operating costs provide greater security for nongovernmental organizations in overcoming a sharp decrease in external project funding that might otherwise jeopardize their existence. In an environment of weak financial controlling, it can be tempting for NGO leaders to take advantage of the "fatter" phases of external funding by arranging for kickbacks and otherwise deviating funds in order to build a base of assets that can be used in "leaner" phases. Foreign sponsors can achieve transparency in such an environment only if their sponsorship policy goes beyond the financing of isolated projects to long-term cooperation that supports the operating expenses of their partner organizations.

The Demonization of Administrative Costs

Another structural weakness that hinders the control of misuse affects relief organizations dependent on private donations to finance their work. In the past, they outdid themselves with attempts at convincing potential donors that none of their donated money would go to administrative costs: "Every penny of your donation reaches the needy!" As long as this assertion only serves to improve the public view of aid organizations, it is irrelevant to the issue of misuse. It becomes problematic when administrative costs are demonized, and as a consequence, the personnel necessary to properly accompany and supervise projects can no longer be guaranteed. Without adequate personnel, a sponsoring organization cannot fulfill its responsibilities. Reasonable limitations on administrative costs are, of course, an important criterion in judging the efficiency of aid organizations. However, becoming a sponsoring organization that can boast about spending little or no money on administration is also not the ultimate goal, especially with regard to misuse control. In an environment marked by corruption and legal insecurity, it is essential to carefully select and monitor projects. In a vast and confusing sector of non-governmental partners, only those who operate in a network with other aid organizations and partners, those who take time for questions, those who consider reports by partners more than just a formality, and those who at least randomly check projects on-site can actually separate the wheat from the chaff. Aid organizations can indeed guarantee that 100 percent of their donations will be spent, but the quality of their administration will influence how efficiently they reach the needy.

Regardless of the aspect of corruption control, demonizing administrative costs, as has been done for decades through the competition for donations among aid organizations, is not a useful strategy in eradicating the prejudice that most donations are spent on administrative costs anyway. A simple statement as to what percentage of aid provided is spent on administration would soothe the nerves of many donors far more than general assertions that the money they donate has nothing to do with administrative costs. For many, a simple statement would also mean a surprising correction of their own previous estimates. Recently, more and more aid organizations have begun to publish figures showing their administrative costs.

Notes

1. See, for example, OECD (1993); NORAD (2000), p. 33; Court of Auditors (2000), clause 33.

2. See Langerbein (2000), pp. 34ff, on several sub-Saharan countries.

3. Ibid. (2000), p. 36.

4. On private donations, see German Federal Government (1994). On the issue of timely utilization, see, in particular, clause 42, p. 29.

5. See Cremer (1996), pp. 172ff.

6. See Cremer (2002).

7. In addition, disbursement pressure raises the costs of disaster relief during an acute phase. This inevitably has negative consequences for the ability of NGOs to finance long-term programs of reconstruction while the media focus turns to the next disaster.

8. See Jessen (1994), pp. 53ff; Sinaga (1994), pp. 100ff. The degree of dependence on external sources varies. Citing NGOs in Thailand as an example, Jessen (1994) points to efforts by some organizations to diversify their financial sources. The chances for success are significantly higher in a fast-developing nation like Thailand than in low-income countries.

11

Corruption in Project Work: An Analysis of Weakness

THIS CHAPTER SUMMARIZES THE PREVIOUS CHAPTERS IN THE form of a list. A weakness analysis is an instrument well known from programs designed to control corruption in the public sector.[1] A list should enable managers to judge where certain risks lie and where a more detailed investigation might be appropriate. Having said that, the sheer presence of one or more weak points does not necessarily mean corrupt activity will occur. The weakness analysis can only provide hints as to where dangers might arise, perhaps because it is particularly difficult for people in charge to implement controls, or because structural forces exist that leave the people involved with no choice but to maneuver outside of the legal realm. The weakness analysis alone does not prove anything. However, it is a useful tool for corruption control. In the following sections, the terms *implementing partner* or *implementing organization* refer to state or NGOs responsible for project implementation in developing countries.

Prerequisites for Project Evaluation

• Is there a clear definition of the project goal? Are the project's target groups and the expected project results clearly defined? Will it thus be at all possible to recognize grave deviations during the project implementation phase?

• What sources of information can the donor tap to gain insights into project implementation and project results? Is she completely dependent on reports from the implementing partner, or does she have access to other, independent sources of information? For instance, does she have the option of directly contacting the target group herself?

• Is the target group aware of the services they can expect to receive from the project? Are representatives of the target group integrated into controlling the project?

• Is the donor informed about local prices so that she can check the plausibility of prices listed in project budgeting and in financial reports? Or would it instead be possible to artificially raise budget numbers in order to conceal misappropriation? In such a case, misappropriation would not inevitably result in differences between project planning and project outcome.

• Does the manager of the implementing organization have access to adequate sources of information to realistically evaluate the work of those carrying out the project on location?

• To what extent do systematic barriers to the flow of information exist? Are there disadvantages for the staff of either the funding or the implementing organization if they pass on evidence of misuse?

• Are there instruments available to the financial supporter that enable her to observe and assess the long-term effects of a project, even following its official completion? Could she retroactively establish misuse that has been skillfully disguised by administrative maneuvering? Would the donor take the next logical steps in future dealings with the implementing partner?

Conditions for Controlling Finances

• What external control structures exist in the project country? Is the implementing organization subject to legal requirements for the transparent billing of accounts? What risks of prosecution accompany methods of "creative" bookkeeping in the project country?

• To what extent is it common in the project country for suppliers to overbill or to otherwise manipulate receipts in order to cooperate in a misappropriation scam?

• Is funding coming in from other donors? If so, are corresponding donations transparent? Can one exclude the possibility that project expenses are billed twice to two separate donors?

• How are funds transferred to the partner organization? Has the currency exchange rate been confirmed by the partner's own paperwork or by an official bank document? Is there an active black market parallel to the official foreign exchange market that tempts partners to exchange funds illicitly in order to secure misappropriation? Are funds transferred to countries with high inflation rates in installments related to the progress of project implementation?

• What financial controls are used in the implementing organization? Do internal control structures exist?

• Are there necessary separations of power to support controls within the implementing partner? Is the authority to transfer money separate from the authority to carry out financial controls?

• Are contracts with outside parties awarded based on a transparent bidding procedure? Are there regulations that stipulate which monetary amounts require which type of bidding procedure? Does the implementing partner have an internal procedure for controlling the awarding of contracts?

• Are wages within the implementing organization commensurate with staff members' qualifications? Are those wages in alignment with those of the public sector? Is it common there to obtain extralegal additional income?

• Does the project environment force project leaders to make extralegal payments in order to carry out the project (payments for permits, "acceleration money" to speed up red tape processes)? Who makes the decisions regarding such payments? Can they be transparently recorded, or must they be disguised within the bookkeeping system?

Project Designs Susceptible to Abuse

• Are extensive outside contracting and procuring a part of the project? Does procurement involve standardized goods (for which it is easy to establish the local market price) or project-specific goods, including custom-built products?

• Is there evidence of purchases that do not fit the purpose of the project? Are expensive, technically difficult investments transacted, even though easier alternatives were available?

• Do disbursement pressures, in particular deadlines for expending project funds, diminish negotiating leverage with commercial suppliers, such as when improvements are required following contract completion?

Relations Between Donors and Implementing Partners

• Is there a long-standing relationship between the donor and the implementing partner? In the case of misuse, will the partner lose access to external donations in current or in future projects or face a reduction?

• How does the implementing partner finance its administrative costs? Is this financing transparent, that is, has it been openly agreed upon by both the donor and the partner? Does any deviation of funds serve to finance administrative costs not officially covered?

• Does the donor act under disbursement pressure? Do her employees suffer disadvantages if completion of the project as agreed is delayed due to an investigation into evidence of misuse?

• Does the implementing partner act under disbursement pressure? How strict are deadlines for expending funds? Does the partner have a margin for altering project plans or delaying implementation if that is required by a reaction to evidence relevant to misuse?

• Which criteria does the donor apply in assessing the performance ability of the implementing partner? Is any deviation of project implementation from the project plan considered an indication that the partner is "weak," did a poor job of planning, and so on? In light of such a performance evaluation, would it be rational for an implementing partner to adhere to project implementation despite evidence pointing to misuse?

• Is it possible to openly discuss the issue of controlling misuse when a donor and a partner organization meet to arrange for, accompany, and evaluate the project?

Note

1. For an example, see the Internal Control Guidelines of the Office of Management and Budget, Washington, DC, described in Klitgaard (1988), pp. 84–85.

12

Confronting the Challenges

FOR A LONG TIME, BOTH STATE-RUN AND NONGOVERNmental development aid organizations simply ignored the fact that they support projects in an environment where corruption is an everyday phenomenon. Even though their funds had been expended via the government bodies of recipient countries where making extralegal additional income is the order of the day, development aid organizations declared themselves untouched by corruption. Since former president James Wolfensohn assumed his post in 1995, the World Bank has made a central issue of corruption, both as an obstacle to development and as a problem that affects the project work of the World Bank itself. This has become a lasting change in policy. With such conceptual leadership by the World Bank, bilateral donors will not be able to avoid thinking about how their funding might foster corrupt practices in recipient countries and which policy of corruption control they should pursue. The breakdown of taboos that goes hand in hand with the above is essential to making substantial progress with corruption control.

Taboos create barriers to the flow of information. As long as a donor organization proclaims—due to whatever secret powers—that its work is to remain free from corruption, it is not opportune for its employees to register evidence that constitutes misuse and to convey that knowledge to the leaders of their organization. Under the circumstances of taboo, employees will at least refrain from perceiving or passing on such information when the signals that point to corruption can at best only vaguely be perceived. A certain interest in detective work is required of an employee in a donor organization before he can derive real suspicion from various signals such as overpricing, contradictions within reports, impressions from project visits that contradict reported success, and skeptical remarks by individuals representing the target group. As long as the leaders in a donor organization make a taboo out of corruption and in doing so send clear signals that they do not want to receive any information about it, every staff member not personally interested in detective work is spared the trouble of reporting. Employees can rest assured that everything is in order, or that at least nothing can be proved to the contrary. As soon as a staff member knows "too much," he faces the dilemma of whether to pass on information to people higher up who do not want to hear it anyway, or to keep it to himself and thus risk being accused of having concealed information from his superior should corrupt practices become evident in his project area despite all taboos.

Training Employees to Recognize and Respond to Corruption

If the taboo is broken, it is also possible to integrate the issue of corruption in development cooperation into the training of development workers, experts, and administrative staff members of development aid organizations. As far as I know, that is seldom done. When development workers or experts leave for their target country, they are generally unprepared for their first direct experience with corruption occurrences, which leaves them feeling uncertain:

- How should aid workers or experts conduct themselves when, as project leaders, they are asked by outsiders to make extralegal payments and, in refusing, have to accept project-related or personal disadvantages?
- How do they recognize evidence of misuse in their own projects?
- How should they react to staff activities that are illegitimate by standards of their country of origin but acceptable in the project country?
- How can they decide where to start when they want to provide for more transparency within their own projects?
- What risks do they run in investigating evidence of misuse, for example, when they discover that the building done for a project does not meet the standards stipulated by the contract?[1]

Usually, they are unprepared for such situations. As long as these problems are not openly discussed during preparation for a project assignment, they may be reluctant to seek advice from superiors or coworkers in the dispatching office. Yet the conditions could be right for allaying uncertainties: There are staff members within development organizations who have experienced corruption in their own project work, who are in a position to explain risky situations using firsthand examples, and who could be useful in the training of future workers.

Dealing with the Public in New Ways

The breakdown of taboos should not be limited to communication within development aid organizations. It requires changes in the way organizations deal with the public. As soon as evidence of corruption is talked about, as soon as guidelines for conduct have been established, staff members will speak more openly about corruption, and journalists specializing in this field will share in knowledge pertaining to corruption. One reason aid organizations swept the problem of corruption under the carpet for such a long time was their desire to present aid work to the public, to taxpayers, and to private donors in the very best light possible. However, aid organizations have no monopoly over public information regarding their work. The public is exposed to contradictory messages: a frequently distorted optimistic image that aid organizations believe they should spread, as well as an equally distorted image disseminated by the media that tends to accentuate any failed aid program for its sensational entertainment value.[2] It would be easier for the public to get a realistic picture if aid organizations themselves took the initiative to point out the risks their work entails. Simultaneously, aid organizations could provide information about the tools they employ to limit corruption, even under unfavorable conditions. Such a realistic way of dealing with the public would presumably not result in a decline in public support for development aid.

Having said that, aid organizations should certainly avoid painting themselves into a corner by burdening their own control policies with unrealistically high expectations. The chances of avoiding corruption by means of "strict measures of protection and control" (as postulated by the German federal government) are just as limited as with any other form of crime: Its occurrence can be diminished but not eradicated.[3] Even with improved control policies and far-reaching administrative and political reform, corruption will occur in developing countries and development aid; if control measures are successful, it will occur at a lower level. But it will continue to occur, just as corruption occurs in industrialized countries within parts of public administration despite incomparably more favorable circumstances, functioning criminal prosecution systems, and wages commensurate with qualifications. It is not new for aid organizations to burden themselves with unrealistic obligations. Their claim to overcoming mass poverty in developing countries may have had appeal, but it remains a claim that development aid simply cannot make good on because of its limited quantitative scope and its lesser significance in comparison to other factors. However, since taxpayers and private donors cannot be blind to the fact that mass poverty still exists after several decades of development aid, the appeal turns into an inquiry as to the legitimacy of development cooperation. The same is to be expected when aid organizations promise too much success with their corruption control policies.

Avoiding Crusades

As soon as one recognizes that the risk of corruption in development aid is, to varying degrees and relative to circumstances, inevitable, corruption control can be considered a way of striving for gradual improvement rather than the path to a final solution. Corruption control is a job that never ends. Even if control procedures are improved, they can be circumvented by new methods of deviating funds. The creativity shown by corrupt officials cannot always be anticipated, not even by the best control policies. Costs are attached to every form of control, including direct costs (for control staff) and indirect costs (the bureaucratization tied to additional control procedures). One can also assume that with increasing expenditure, returns in the form of avoided direct and indirect damage by corruption will decrease, and starting at a certain point, the damage done by rigid control will dominate. Another reason why corruption control never fully succeeds is because it is carried out in surroundings of unfavorable institutional conditions. Therefore, any type of crusade mentality should be avoided. Any claims that development aid should be "corruption-free" and any loud-mouthed announcement of zero tolerance principles would only contribute to the establishment of new taboos. If such claims were taken seriously, all cooperation with government bodies and most nongovernmental institutions in many countries, particularly in poorly performing states, would have to be stopped.[4] That would, however, contradict the institutional interest of development aid organizations, and they would try to steer clear of such a situation by ignoring evidence of corruption as long as possible. Brian Cooksey is basically right in establishing that "aid agencies are reluctant to apply their formal 'zero tolerance' principles in practice, and may consequently ignore or deny evidence of systemic corruption, including the misuse of their own programme or project funds."[5] But the point he makes supports the formulation of a somewhat more modest term than *zero tolerance* for defining corruption control objectives in development aid. The core of the matter is not "purity," but rather the use of development cooperation as a tool to contribute to reform and increased transparency in recipient countries. The goal of corruption control is secondary to the goal of development, and it is of instrumental character in pursuing this goal because the effects of corruption are, on the whole, hostile to development.

Improving the Empirical Base

For a long time corruption was regarded as a social phenomenon that could not at all be researched empirically or, if so, only with many restrictions. Arrangements for bribery or misappropriation scams are made in secret. Direct observation is not possible, and the people involved are not necessarily willing to answer inquiries. However, these obstacles are by no means insurmountable. Recent studies show that corporate managers and even public officials will talk about evidence of corruption in their field of work if they do not have to reveal any criminally relevant details of their arrangements and if their anonymity is preserved in analysis.[6] Surveys of development workers and experts could gather empirical information about corruption phenomena in development aid. Such surveys should preferably be done by institutions acting independently of dispatching organizations in order to ensure the confidentiality of individual statements and could include some of the following questions.

- Was extralegal income common in their project surroundings?
- Did they perceive large discrepancies between the legal wages

of public or nongovernmental staff members and the expenditures necessary to support the lifestyles those people led?

- Have they noticed, in the course of goods procurement for projects, substantial differences between prices listed in project paperwork and actual market prices?
- What degree of reliability would they attach to the bidding procedures being used?
- How would they assess the financial management of their partner organization?
- Were internal control structures in place in the partner organization?
- Were target group members aware of the services they were to receive through the project?
- Do they suspect that the project-planning phase had already been influenced by the intent to secure misappropriation with the least possible risk?

Of course, most of these questions can be answered only with the aid of a rating scale. However, most respondents give a subjective rating based on many years of everyday experience. Subjective as they may be, such observations are not irrelevant. Systematic surveys of aid workers and experts could provide important corruption-related information about differences between countries, project types, and partner groups. Such information might help in deciding where corruption control measures are most urgently needed or in determining which types of projects might carry special risks.

There are further empirical sources that remain essentially untapped. Case studies on individual projects or programs can give detailed insights into interrelations among the political and social surroundings of a project, structures of a partner organization, project design, and corruption risks. Such case studies can be written when aid organizations open project files to external scientists and permit them to evaluate a project, including any aspects of misuse, and to talk at length with staff members. An agreement could be made to keep information anonymous in the publicized version of the case study in order to avoid exposing any partner organization that is most likely conducting itself no differently from the majority of other recipient organizations in the same country. After all, it is not the goal of a case study to turn individual stories into scandals, but rather to gain deep insight into a system that supports the deviation of funds and to create improved conditions for corruption control. Any lack of meaningful case studies in this field is a result of aid organizations shielding their work from outsiders. The empirical base could also be expanded if regular project evaluations, which are carried out in great numbers, required assessments of corruption risks and reports on evidence pointing to misappropriation. In addition, aid workers and experts will be willing to talk or write about their experiences with corruption as soon as aid organizations stop treating the topic as taboo.

Effectiveness-Centered Control

As discussed earlier, corruption control that relies primarily on administrative regulations is limited in its effectiveness if officials can manipulate the documents and procedures it relies on. An external donor does not have the authority necessary to carry out an independent investigation. Generally, he is not in a position to check out businesses that have obviously overcharged for services, thus making themselves look suspicious as an accessory to misappropriation in the form of a kickback. If institutions in recipient countries, such as tax or auditing authorities, do not have the power to make inquiries or do not exercise that power, then control mechanisms based on such procedures will not suffice. However, an external donor does have the power to assess the effectiveness of projects. Extensive misappropriation schemes are compatible with project goals only when the officials involved anticipated their intended illegal profits during the budget planning phase and included them by significantly overestimating certain budget items. If manipulation of budget items could be prevented, one could infer from a lack of any grave differences between plan and actual implementation, both quantitatively and qualitatively, that no large-scale misappropriation took place during project implementation. However, grave discrepancies between planned and real outcomes do not constitute proof of misappropriation. They can arise from unrealistic and thus unattainable project goals, from hostile circumstances, or from deficits in project implementation that can occur without legal violation. However, grave discrepancies do provide grounds for suspicion. If a project partner is responsible for grave discrepancies, his foreign donor—if he has the liberty to do so and if other measures were not successful—can impose sanctions on the recipient by refusing or decreasing further aid. In doing so, the donor does not have to justify his actions by citing his suspicion of misuse of project funds. He generally does not have sufficient evidence anyway. Rather, he can justify his actions by pointing to deficits in project implementation, independent of whether the deficits stem from misuse or, for instance, from poor management. Sanction mechanisms that are based on effectiveness-centered project controls can create incentives for project partners to check misuse, even in situations in which administrative control procedures fall short.

Including Anticorruption Clauses

It has become standard in recent international agreements on development cooperation for contractual partners to commit to cooperating on corruption control. The inclusion of an explicit anticorruption clause goes back to a May 1996 recommendation by the OECD Development Assistance Committee.[7] Since then, many donor countries have followed suit.[8] A clause like that one has no immediate impact because even governments whose members participate in graft themselves and have no intention of changing their ways will sign. The World Bank, which was the first significant donor to admit that its own projects were vulnerable to country-specific corruption risks, encourages its borrowers to require bidders and potential contractors to sign an anticorruption clause during the bidding phase. However, the World Bank goes one step further than the OECD Development Assistance Committee by obliging borrowing countries to introduce procedures acceptable to the Bank that allow for reporting of corrupt practices.[9] In particular, bidders who received no contract because a co-competitor bribed officials in charge would be considered potential informants.

Anticorruption clauses are often only a "symbol to create awareness" that might be helpful to initiate discussion with partners about corruption.[10] They can truly be effective only if donors make it clear that they are prepared to break with past traditions of ignoring evidence of corruption and if such clauses are one component of an integrated corruption control policy that goes beyond mere symbols.

Improving Procurement Procedures

The World Bank has taken the initiative to go beyond the symbolic. Due to the quantitative significance of its loans for many recipient countries, the Bank is in a far better position than bilateral donors to set conditions in its lending policy and to require certain control procedures. Through joint initiatives on corruption control, the Bank and bilateral donors could concentrate the power of their donations to achieve anticorruption goals. One focus taken by the World Bank to prevent corruption in its own projects lies in the area of procurement and the design of bidding procedures. If bidding procedures are grossly manipulated, it is possible to secure extensive misappropriation schemes via kickback arrangements. Following James Wolfensohn's initial venture, the World Bank expanded its procurement guidelines to include a paragraph on "Fraud and Corruption."[11] The Bank now threatens to withdraw loan approvals if it ascertains that officials working for a borrower commit corruption or fraud during bidding procedures or project implementation. If a borrower takes no counteraction deemed satisfactory by the Bank, it reserves the right to recall the part of an approved loan that was earmarked for the goods and services whose procurement involved irregularities. The Bank has announced that loan approval will be withdrawn from the start if the recommended contractor is found to have influenced the bidding procedure through corrupt activity.

Of course, the threat to recall an approved loan can have an impact only if the World Bank obtains sufficient evidence of corrupt or fraudulent activity. For that reason, the Bank endeavors to improve its access to such evidence. Since its procurement guidelines have been revised, the Bank insists on its right to see the accounts and books of contractors working on projects financed by the World Bank and to select and hire an auditor to check financial records.[12] In comparison with an audit that is restricted to the financial records of the borrower, a look into contractors' books improves the chances of revealing kickback arrangements. As discussed earlier, corrupt officials have seen an advantage in this type of arrangement, as compared with other forms of misappropriation, because they can shift the resulting bookkeeping problem onto the contractor. Now, however, the contractor's books can also be subject to an audit, a step forward that makes it more difficult to arrange a kickback. However, under certain conditions the effect will be limited, if contractors make arrangements with their suppliers to manipulate receipts, thus leaving a World Bank auditor empty-handed.

The World Bank now also has a new requirement for bidding documents: They must show proof of commission payments to agents. That is important because the parties involved in corruption contracts often make use of a liaison between officials and companies. Middlemen are popular for two reasons: (1) They diminish the risk of disclosure linked to the search for and communication with potential partners in corrupt agreements; and (2) they accumulate experience and knowledge from working on a number of corrupt contracts and are thus able to tell contractors what kind of payments are common in any given area. If an agent is used in a bribe, then the bribe money is not paid by the actual briber but rather by the agent, who pays the bribe money from the total fee given to him. If the fee paid to an agent is substantially higher than the amount commensurate with his actual service, there is strong evidence that officials are bribed via middlemen.[13] In alignment with such occurrences, Transparency International has developed an "Integrity Pact" between governments and contractors that provides for the disclosure of payments to agents and other middlemen made during the bidding process or during the phase of project implementation.[14]

One indicator of kickbacks is a large discrepancy between the price settled upon for a contract in a manipulated bidding process and prices for comparable contracts in the private sector. Comparing prices among government projects alone is of very limited use if kickback arrangements are common in the government sector. A very preliminary attempt at comparing contract prices for similar goods in publicly and privately financed projects in Indonesia showed discrepancies of between 15 percent and 40 percent.[15] A system of comparing prices that is based solely on government projects would only serve to prevent misappropriation on a level above the common range. However, the comparison of prices independent of the government sector, prices for goods or parts of projects that can be standardized, can be helpful to donors investigating large-scale kickback arrangements.

But even if the price settled on does not deviate greatly from a price fixed in a properly executed bidding procedure, one cannot exclude the possibility that contractors and officials have arranged for a kickback. Because the contractor cannot finance a kickback through excessive earnings, he will take advantage of opportunities to reduce quantity or quality standards. Earlier in the book, I defined that practice as a "modified kickback." It can be restricted only by improved supervision of the physical implementation of projects.

Creating Risks for Corrupt Contractors

It is not just companies in recipient countries that benefit from large aid projects. Companies in Western donor countries also participate. Since the enactment of the OECD convention, the bribery of a foreign official has become a criminal offense in important donor countries if the aim of the bribe is to achieve an unjust advantage or to secure a contract in international business dealings (see Chapter 6).

Civil sanctions may also increase risks for corrupt contractors, especially if companies that have been found guilty of bribery or fraud or attempted bribery or fraud with the intention of securing a contract are excluded either temporarily or indefinitely from receiving any further contracts. In its procurement guidelines, the World Bank threatens companies participating in bidding for or implementing World Bank projects with the possibility of such sanctions.[16] Because this threat not only refers to the country in which fraud and corruption have been proven but is valid around the globe, it sends a very powerful message to companies active in the international development business. In November 1998 the World Bank formed a sanctions committee that, following investigations by the Bank's Oversight Committee on Fraud and Corruption (and since 2000 by a new independent department, called the Department of Institutional Integrity) makes recommendations to the president to prohibit individuals or companies from participating in World Bank projects for a limited or indefinite time.[17] As of January 1, 2008, the "World Bank Listing of Ineligible Firms (Fraud and Corruption)" included 123 firms. This list is available on the World Bank homepage, accessible to anyone at any time. Forty-seven of the firms listed to date have been banned for a limited time (mostly three to five years), most of them because they were found guilty of fraudulent practices such as the "misrepresentation" of facts in order to influence a procurement process or of collusive practices among bidders designated to establish bid prices at noncompetitive levels. This information is much easier to trace than the bribery of officials in recipient countries. Seventy-six firms have been banned permanently. In nearly all cases the bribing of public officials in the procurement process or in contract execution constituted grounds for a permanent ban.[18] Out of 115 firms and individuals sanctioned in fiscal years 2005 and 2006, sixty-nine were from Indonesia.[19] For a long time in Indonesia, corruption in government procurement was so common that firms did not even apply the most basic methods to cover up illicit behavior, which makes it easy for World Bank auditors to uncover these maneuvers. It remains to be seen whether the auditors will still be successful when firms learn to disguise their illicit practices better than in the past.

In addition to the disqualified companies listed, the sanctions also apply to companies in which the disqualified companies hold a majority of stock, as well as companies that hold a majority of stock in one of the disqualified companies.[20] That rule prevents the guilty from establishing new companies or operations with others as their "fronts."[21]

A debarment policy can serve as an important part of a properly organized procurement process. The debarment process must meet appropriate standards to avoid the risk of misuse as a political tool or to keep competing companies from falsely complaining about corruption. A properly resourced investigative process, procedures, and criteria for establishing guilt and opportunities to challenge the evidence are needed.[22] Individual bilateral donors who do not have the same clout as the World Bank could nonetheless increase risks for corrupt contractors and reduce the spread of bribery and kickback arrangements in development aid by working jointly on a blacklisting procedure for corrupt contractors or even reaching joint agreements with the World Bank and other multilateral donors.[23]

Integrating Target Groups into Control Systems

Corruption control prescribed externally by donors does not suffice. Because corruption in development aid usually harms target groups who consequentially do not receive aid at all, receive it too late, or receive goods of poor quality, target groups generally have an interest in contributing to corruption control. Surveys of target groups or their representatives can reveal whether services were provided as planned or were only provided in exchange for extralegal payments. Surveys can also give clues about corrupt activities occurring at the lowest executive level of a project.[24] Surveys of target groups should thus be considered a core element of effectiveness-centered control that complements administrative control regulations. Carrying out these surveys is, however, more difficult than it appears: They have to be carried out independent of local governing bodies that are the object of control. In authoritarian political systems and under circumstances of legal insecurity, the consequences for those who respond to surveys are difficult to predict, should they make incriminating remarks about the local administration. Instead of improving their situation, their complaints may result in sanctions imposed by officials whom they depend on for the receipt of other government services as well.[25] In such situations, target group members will be careful or very vague in making statements, unless they are part of an organized group able to defend itself.

Corruption control aided by target groups is greatly improved when service delivery is transparent, that is, when it is clear which groups are entitled to which services and which services were made available to whom. It is particularly important when project implementation includes the distribution of goods, because in that case local officials might not distribute all goods but rather sell some to dealers or pass them on to others not entitled to those goods in exchange for personal gain. The field of relief aid offers experience in making the distribution of goods transparent to the local community. Local church-related partners have often organized the distribution of relief goods as a public event. Goods are passed out at a previously announced time on a public square. Everyone can watch and see who receives what amount. Because the local watchful eye is very well informed about the social and economic situation of each recipient—far better anyway than a local functionary or the representative of an aid organization—this procedure limits opportunities for misuse. It also furnishes protection against allegations that even honest local organizations are subject to in countries where corruption is a common occurrence and where every activity that could be used as a source of extralegal income is viewed with suspicion. Corruption control can be taken one step further by integrating target group representatives into the planning and implementation phases of a project. It is feasible to have representatives of target groups or civil organizations acting in the interest of target groups participate in decisions about the awarding of contracts.[26] Under conditions of systematic corruption, there is, of course, always the danger that representatives have been involved in manipulating the bidding procedure and have gained from a kickback themselves, thus making it impossible for them to do justice to their role in controlling corruption.

Requiring Anticorruption Structures in NGO Project Sponsorship

Development cooperation between states inevitably depends on cooperation with governing bodies as they stand. A financial donor as powerful as the World Bank, backed by the weight of its loan approvals, can effect changes in the public sector of a recipient country, and bilateral donors, in a concerted effort, could do so as well. However, a greater degree of transparency and control of misuse in development cooperation with government bodies cannot, in the end, be attained in isolation. It must be one component of reform of the public service sector in recipient countries.

Success is less difficult to come by in cooperating with nongovernmental organizations. As mentioned earlier, the top people in NGOs hold a position of trust that they can misuse for private gains, just as government officials do. In contrast to public officials, however, NGO officers do not have a monopoly in their field of work; rather, they usually have to compete for foreign funding with a number of other NGOs. Donors thus have leverage in deciding which potential partner they want to support and how to design cooperation. They can demand transparency from nongovernmental organizations. Donors consequently bear partial responsibility for ensuring that the NGO sector is more than just a self-organized form of obtaining extralegal advantages for people who could not make it into public service.

External donors who take this responsibility seriously will not limit their work to isolated projects but will integrate project work into long-term cooperation, including the establishment and improvement of structures within their partner organizations. External donors must insist that their partner organizations maintain a supervisory committee that determines organization policies (including binding working procedures) and oversees the manager and the staff. Such "committees of responsibility" are often lacking among the many NGOs founded in reaction to offers of foreign funding. To my knowledge, it is common for decisionmaking powers in NGOs in developing countries to be concentrated in the hands of employees who decide which projects deserve funding, who simultaneously act as project leaders and bear responsibility for implementation, and who—without further supervision—also write or approve final project reports. In the end it is not possible to effectively check misuse under such circumstances.

The establishment of supervisory committees independent of the people responsible for operations constitutes the basic requirement for more transparency in the NGO sector. Only external donors who commit themselves to lasting relations beyond the funding of individual projects will be able to promote structural changes in their partner organizations. Only they can urge partner organizations to professionalize their financial management if their partners do not do so on their own initiative. Such changes can be effected more smoothly if managers in partner organizations realize that professional financial management does not just help external donors carry out controls; it also provides the conditions necessary for managers to steer project work and development within their own organizations.

There are other reasons why donors supporting NGOs can improve conditions for supporting anticorruption structures if they enter into a long-term partnership with their NGO partners. In long-term relationships the external sponsor can more readily assess his partner's performance and judge the extent to which his partner is able to establish (or intends to establish) corruption control within a local organization. Here, the sustainability of a project is a significant indirect indicator. Large-scale misappropriation has a negative effect on the endurance of a project. This is plain to see in long-term investments like buildings because quality decreases where misappropriation is at work. Negative consequences are not necessarily noticed at the time construction is completed or when a project ends. They often surface years later. The endurance of a project can also suffer when essential project steps have been invoiced (e.g., motivating and training a target group) but have only occurred on paper. If a sponsor has no long-standing relations with project partners, the project he once sponsored will quickly disappear from his world. At the time a sponsor closes his end of the deal, it is difficult to predict whether a project will have lasting effects or whether it will have improved the situation of target groups in the long run. A lack of permanence in relations between external sponsors and their partners bears negative consequences for corruption control as well. In addition, given a lasting commitment, the leaders within a partner organization calculate risks differently because each and every corruption offense jeopardizes long-term cooperation and can thus be very expensive for the partner organization. And finally, external sponsors and partners in a long-term relationship have greater chances of shaping their relations so as to make it unnecessary for the partner organization to employ kickbacks or other methods of deviating funds in order to comply with its legitimate institutional interests.

In addition, only external donors who build on lasting cooperation can create conditions in their partner organizations that allow for any transparency at all. This entails building up an organization that can pay its employees wages commensurate with their qualifications. The form of payment may differ. Guaranteed salaries can be complemented by additional income, depending on the size of a project. Such additional income would not contradict the goal of limiting misuse if it is agreed upon in a transparent manner and checked by a supervisory committee separate from the staff. Through control procedures and a system of accountability, the organization can prove that it will not tolerate extralegal additional income, which would no longer be necessary or legitimate. Transparency requires clear-cut regulations on how a partner organization covers its basic administrative costs. If no such regulations exist, administrative costs are often covered by deviating funds in ways very similar to the procedures used to secure misappropriation for private gains. If the survival of an organization depends on such procedures because legal mechanisms for financing structural costs are lacking, managers will do all they can to resist more transparency.

Donor responsibility for the level of misuse control in partner organizations is also related to project funding itself. Funding must be based on a project agreement or, in the case of long-term relations, on a broader foundation of agreed-upon conditions that define the rights and obligations of both sides and that give local partners confidence in working with requirements tied to funding. Such terms include decisionmaking processes for adapting a project budget to new, unforeseen circumstances or rules concerning reporting, auditing, and other financial issues. External auditing should become the standard, even among nongovernmental organizations. In addition, conditions should be set on decisionmaking for the procurement of goods, on the registration of capital goods, and on how they should be sold. NGO projects also award contracts of substantial volume in which the risk of kickback arrangements runs high if there are no fixed procedures for procurement and no rules governing decisionmaking responsibilities.

In determining the details of such rules and conditions, one has to consider the differences among the legal situations in recipient countries. NGOs in developing countries that are supported by several donors complain about the additional bureaucratic expenditure they must face in producing reports for various donors in varying formats and with varying due dates. These complaints should be taken seriously. It is not a matter of setting a global standard for each administrative detail. It is a matter of pushing through some very basic rules that will secure transparency in project decisionmaking and in the use of funds.[27]

Cutting Off Aid

What if all attempts at establishing regulations for transparency are in vain, especially because officials have absolutely no interest in them? What if nongovernmental organizations show no willingness whatsoever in talking about the structural aspects of their work as part of project support? Then external donors are left with the one final option of using funds as an instrument of sanction and either reducing or terminating aid.

That should be possible as long as donor organizations do not act under disbursement pressure or insist on upholding donations out of other institutional interests, despite refusals by NGOs to establish transparent systems. For instance, an external nongovernmental donor has one very powerful institutional interest if the partner in question has played a large role in public relations. In ending relations with that partner, the donor organization may fear setbacks in its income from donations. However, since there is no monopoly among NGOs, many possibilities exist for foreign donors to find other partners with whom they might be able to achieve transparency and at the same time preserve their institutional interests.

External donors should take advantage of such possibilities for reasons of self-respect. After all, cooperation with NGOs in developing countries only makes sense if one can trust that the proclaimed development policy or humanitarian goals of the local partner do not simply serve to veil a system for deviating funds. A relationship of trust originates and grows with the willingness of the partner organization to work toward transparency in cooperation with the foreign donor. Then external donors and local partners can also work together on how to limit misuse. Wherever trust cannot be built—either because the local partner hides information pertinent to evaluating the utilization of funds, or because the local partner refuses to talk about its work structures, or because the local partner steers evaluations in such a way that no one can gain insight into project reality—there is no basis for further cooperation. External donors are then obliged, for reasons of misuse control, to give other organizations a chance to work toward transparency.

In the areas of development cooperation between states and of multilateral funding, the obstacles to terminating aid are higher than in cooperation between NGOs. Cutting off aid brings with it the disturbance of political relations. A donor as powerful as the World Bank also has to consider the impact of its decisions on the economic situation and, consequently, on the political stability of the recipient country, especially because a World Bank decision to break off cooperation would give a signal to bilateral donors, multiplying its effect. Thus for countries that are highly dependent on the transfer of development aid, a threat to reduce or cut off aid can be very effective in pushing through reforms in the public service sector and, in particular, in the area of corruption control.

During the long period when corruption problems were taboo, terminating aid as a reaction to evidence of corruption was an extremely rare occurrence. In Cold War days it would not have been compatible with the use of development aid as an instrument in the competition of political systems. As late as 1997, the federal government of Germany made this statement about German development aid: "No development cooperation contracts were annulled due to proof of corruption."[28] The German government, in alignment with its position at that time and following the tradition of taboo, attributed that result to adherence to strict control mechanisms. The German government tried to make the public believe that these mechanisms functioned in cooperation with about 100 countries and so perfectly for several decades that no one ever questioned whether funding should be recalled due to proof of a serious corruption offense.

Back in 1993, more than two years before Wolfensohn took office, the World Bank cut off its credit relationship with Zaire because corruption in Bank-sponsored projects was excessive. The Bank did not, however, openly state the reason for breaking off loan relations. In the second half of the 1990s, the World Bank halted projects in Nigeria, Sudan, Congo, and Afghanistan as a reaction to evidence of corruption. In those cases, the reasons were no secret.[29] Today Bank guidelines include the threat to recall loans, or part of them, if officials in a recipient country misuse funds and the government does not take any countermeasures that satisfy the Bank. Although it does publish a list of firms found guilty of fraud and corruption, the World Bank is not very forthcoming to the public as to how often it recalls loans. When the World Bank began to threaten to recall loans, critics assumed that recall would most likely hit poorer, smaller, and politically less influential countries because the political trouble the World Bank would have to face in such cases is negligible. By comparison, the Bank would probably shy away from reacting similarly in its relations with China.[30] That assumption is still very plausible today, but because the World Bank is rather reluctant to communicate details of its loan recall policy, the empirical basis for proving this assumption is weak. It is also plausible to expect that bilateral donors who follow the example of the World Bank and threaten to recall loans in order to combat corruption also will shrink away from sanctioning governments of politically important countries.

The World Bank uses its instrument of recall as a type of partial sanction.[31] The current procurement guidelines announce that the Bank will "cancel that portion of the loan allocated to the goods and works that have been misprocured" or "allocated to a contract if it determines at any time that representatives of the Borrower or of a beneficiary of the loan engaged in corrupt, fraudulent, collusive, or coercive practices during the procurement or the execution of that contract, without the Borrower having taken timely and appropriate action satisfactory to the Bank to address such practices when they occur."[32] At first glance, restricting part of a loan appears less threatening than cutting off cooperation altogether. At the same time, this gradual process increases the chances that recall of financing will be used as a tool for control in development aid. The obstacle of deciding, on the part of the World Bank or even on the part of all donors, to cut off cooperation completely would be insurmountable with regard to countries with which political relations are meant to continue.

By contrast, breaking off one single project or recalling part of a loan represents measures that can be precisely steered and effectively implemented. Donors can send a clear signal that they have seriously committed themselves to corruption control and that they expect borrowing countries to take further steps to reform the public sector. In the end, a gradual approach is more appropriate than a radical threat without consequences. The World Bank shows its support for a moderate approach when it speaks of *progressively* placing more responsibility for procurement and allocation of funding into the hands of borrowers, with the overall goal of improving financial management within the governments of recipient countries.[33]

If bilateral state donors and nongovernmental donors seriously want to contribute to corruption control, they must employ the threat of recall or termination of funding in cases of severe corruption when partners refuse to take steps toward greater transparency.

The Importance of Sociopolitical Context

Corruption control policies formed by sponsoring organizations will fall short if those organizations limit their efforts to simply ridding their own projects of corrupt activity. Conditions for corruption control could be improved greatly if bribery, misappropriation, and nepotism in the government sector were less epidemic in general than is the case in many recipient countries today, including governmental areas not touched by development cooperation. I am speaking primarily of development cooperation between states in which project implementation is carried out by civil servants in the recipient country. However, it also holds true for nongovernmental aid: If it is common in the governmental sector to arrange for kickbacks when awarding contracts, if local companies even consider such kickbacks a standard service, if no financial authority does regular checks that create risks, and if prosecution can be eluded by paying bribes, then the conditions for corruption control are extremely unfavorable, even in the NGO sector.

Assuming it were possible to check corruption in the limited field of aid projects under such unfavorable conditions, one could still not exclude the possibility of corrupt income being financed by project funds because budget funds can be freed up for corrupt schemes when aid funds come in. Governments can finance measures they had already planned with aid funds and then misappropriate the money they saved at their own discretion.[34] In all cases where aid is disbursed to program or budget support, donors exert less direct influence, and the extent to which aid is affected by corruption depends on the overall level of corruption control in the recipient countries. It depends on whether key institutions like budget departments in ministries of finance, audit institutions, supervisory institutions for public procurement, and the legal system are prepared for and capable of controlling corruption in the process of disbursement of program and budget aid. Therefore, program or budget aid is only suitable if the aforementioned key institutions are strengthened.[35]

Corruption control policy need not be restricted to checking the behavior of public officials, as important as that step is to an encompassing control policy. It is at least as important to reform the manner and scope of state regulation of the economy with the goal of diminishing incentives for bribery and opportunities for misappropriation. It is equally important to strengthen the judicial system, thus raising the risk of prosecution and sentencing for corruption offenders, to check political power, and to strengthen civil institutions as additional controlling bodies.

Reducing State Intrusion in Economic Processes

State regulations set the stage for public officials to offer bribed services, such as issuing licenses, speeding up administrative processes, or letting criminal acts go unpunished. Therefore, the pursuit of corruption control includes reducing state regulations, especially those that serve no legitimate political, economic, or social goals. For example, if domestic companies are no longer required to apply for a production license, public officials will no longer have the power of selecting who gets the license or the power to delay production starting dates. If obstacles to trade are lowered, for example by revoking a ban on certain imports, then there will no longer be any incentive for import firms to circumvent bans by paying bribes to customs officials. If the government ceases intervention in the agricultural market and farmers are released from their obligation to sell products to state buyers at below-market prices, then farmers will be able to sell freely to private traders without having to bribe state inspectors to do so. Because many such forms of state intervention existed or still exist in most developing countries (not least as a result of strategies by government offices to expand their opportunities for bribery), the reduction of such intervention has played an important role in limiting corruption in the public sector. In an environment of excessive state regulation, every attempt at corruption control will fail if it focuses on merely checking public officials in their execution of regulations without diminishing the great incentives for bribery that have been created by those very regulations.[36]

Deregulation reduces incentives for bribery, but no corruption control policy is able to completely avoid incentives for bribery. The state has to set norms, otherwise no social life would be possible. Since the 1980s, developmental thought has focused on policies to decrease the role of the state and to strengthen the private sector. This phase replaced an earlier phase of developmental thought in which the success of development was mainly attributed to state activities. To quote Bruce Bailey: "There appears to be a shift to a more pragmatic view that the state needs to concentrate its activities better, thus becoming more effective, and this means retreating from some areas of action and playing a stronger state role in other areas."[37] Many norms set by the state fulfill generally accepted purposes, including environmental or consumer protection or building regulations that must be enacted to ensure safety. Even following completion of a successful deregulation program, incentives for bribery remain, if at a lower level. The legal framework imperative to the secure production of or trade in goods must carry a guarantee from the state and requires protection against erosion through bribery. Bribery to secure illegal activity could only be eradicated if the threat of punishment for socially undesirable actions were eliminated, but that would result in a society lacking the protection of the law.[38] Even after deregulation policy is set, there remains a need to diminish the bribery of public officials through appropriate control procedures.

Limiting State Action: Reducing Loopholes for Misappropriation

In many developing countries, state action has been expanded far beyond the "classical" state functions. The government not only makes public goods available but is also active in the production of goods that could be provided by private suppliers without reservation. Thus state-owned enterprises produce steel, cement, or other basic materials. State-owned enterprises often serve the political system of patronage. Management positions within state-owned businesses are passed on to high-ranking members of the reigning political party or to influential followers of the government. Those practices have practical effects within the context of corruption when public officials in state-owned enterprises misuse their position of trust by arranging for kickbacks with suppliers in purchasing goods for the enterprise, and thus securing misappropriation. Of course, managers in private businesses can also similarly misuse discretionary powers, but misuse is possible to a greater extent in state-owned enterprises because they are subject to absolutely no or, by comparison, very little control by the market. It is common in many developing countries to secure the market position of state-owned businesses through diverse measures of intervention: (1) restrictions on investments that make it difficult for competitors to produce; (2) restrictions on imports that limit the influx of competing products; (3) regulations that force domestic producers to purchase a part of their input goods on the domestic market and—if there are no competitors on the domestic market—part of their input goods from state-owned enterprises (so-called local content regulations); or (4) requirements for authorities to make their purchases from state-owned businesses. Because of such types of intervention, state-owned enterprises often find it easy to pass on the costs incurred by misappropriation and nepotism to other sectors and to consumers. If there is also a prevailing bad habit of covering deficits from state-owned businesses with state budget money, then systematic corruption does not even jeopardize the existence of state-owned enterprises. It distinguishes them from private companies that are subject to market controls.

Privatizing state-owned businesses and opening domestic markets can limit large-scale embezzlement. The process of privatization itself carries with it high risks of corruption. Indicators for possible corruption are nontransparent procedures of selecting the new company owners, a non-market-based assessment of the value of the company, unjustifiably low and unsafe labor protection requirements, or a lack of requirements on the continuation of production. In the privatization process there are plenty of decisions that are prone to influence by bribe payments by potential new owners.[39]

Paying Higher Wages to Officials?

Even if state regulations that create opportunities for bribery are curtailed and the state withdraws from areas that can be organized by the private sector, a number of state services must remain whose quality depends on whether executive officials work in a proper manner or a corrupt manner. Policies that reduce state intervention can lower the risks of corruption. However, they do not negate the necessity for public sector reforms that aim to limit bribery, misappropriation, and nepotism in those sectors that must remain in public hands.

As discussed earlier, the legal wages public officials receive in many developing countries lie below wages for positions with comparable qualifications in the private sector. The gap is especially wide among public officials at higher levels who have discretionary powers they can misuse to gain additional income through bribery and embezzlement. An increase in legal wages would push the fiscal limit in many developing countries, in particular because the public sector has been greatly expanded. In many countries substantial raises could only be feasible if the number of public officials were simultaneously reduced.

What would change if, following wage reform, officials in public service received wages commensurate with their qualifications? The value of a public service job would rise, and dismissals from public service jobs as a form of punishment for corruption offenses would make a more significant difference in the calculations made by officials. It would be more difficult for officials to justify corruption by deeming it essential to sustaining an "appropriate" lifestyle. Managers would no longer have to tolerate a certain degree of corruption to keep their staff in the public sector. There might possibly be greater acceptance of control mechanisms among civil servants, and perhaps at least some civil servants would be willing to work with controlling authorities. Less collusion between public officials would significantly improve conditions for control measures.[40]

However, an increase in public service wages does not automatically restrict corruption. Further variables have to be changed that are decisive in the calculations of corrupt officials. Public officials who are not hampered by any inner moral resistance would continue to enhance even commensurate wages with extralegal income if it were possible to do so with the same low risk as before. An increase in wages thus only constitutes one component of an anticorruption policy and can only be effective within a comprehensive civil service reform, including effective auditing, merit-based recruitment and promotion, appropriate training, and replacement of corrupt personnel.[41]

Yet in those countries where civil servants are extremely underpaid, raising salaries will be significant. Without improvements in wages, it is difficult to implement control measures; and if it were possible to stop the flow of illegal income through controls alone, one would have to fear a drain of qualified public officials into the private sector.

Framing Reform Policy for the Public Sector

The extent to which reform policy can succeed at all depends on the political framework imposed on the people who implement reform.

What kind of political backing do reforms get? Should reform efforts take place within narrowly defined sectors, such as the efforts to control corruption within the Philippine tax administration under President Ferdinand Marcos[42] or the Indonesian customs administration under President Suharto—attempts that were restricted because corruption was part of a patronage system presided over by the heads of state?[43] Do reformers have the right to probe into all sectors of civil service according to their own assessment of priorities? A further decisive point is whether the agency authorized to carry out controls is politically and operationally independent. Where does the anticorruption agency recruit its staff? Were its staff members formerly employed by the administrative bodies subject to control, and will they rejoin these bodies later, or can they truly work independently?[44] The degree of effectiveness of controlling bodies depends on their rights and legal power. Do they have the right to obtain information, to investigate on their own, to question witnesses, to secure evidence, to use bank information, and to staunch the flow of profits presumably stemming from corruption by, for example, freezing bank accounts? How far up into the administrative hierarchy can controlling bodies make strikes before losing their political backing? Can they maintain political backing even if they reveal networks of corruption that include high-ranking people from the government and influential businesses? The answer depends on the breadth of their support and on the societal forces that support reform, such as new middle classes that do not participate in extralegal favors and whose economic progress has been hindered. Essential also is the exemplary behavior of the anticorruption agency itself, which must act, and be seen to act, in conformity with international human rights norms, operate within the law, and be accountable to the courts.[45]

Setting Priorities

Priority setting is essential to corruption control policy within public institutions in an environment that has been marked by systematic corruption.[46] When setting priorities, one must ask: Which forms of corruption are considered especially damaging to private individuals who have to deal with a public institution? In answering this question, one can make a very conscious decision to give priority to personal blackmail rather than the misappropriation of income. In the attempt at corruption control in the Philippine tax administration under Marcos (mentioned above), widespread blackmail headed the list of priorities: Tax officials obtained payments from taxpayers by threatening to place them in a much higher tax bracket; due to a lack of any possibility for legal recourse, the threat could only be warded off by paying tax officials directly.[47] Or a top priority could be the corrupt behavior most damaging to an institution itself, for example, misappropriation schemes woven into the awarding of public contracts. Priorities can also be determined by practical considerations, targeting among a variety of corrupt activities those cases for which it seems comparatively easy to gather information and for which the evidence acquired will most likely stand the test of a legal trial. In such cases it is of primary importance that sanctions can actually be imposed in order to prove to public officials and to the general public that control policy is to be taken seriously.

In order to set priorities and to plan civil service reform, it is necessary to ascertain and evaluate the various corruption offenses. Under circumstances of systematic corruption it can be a difficult task to the extent that those responsible for corruption control measures generally may not be insiders in the organizations in question. They should come from the outside so as not to be involved in any existing groups. The result is a serious information problem. In taking stock and evaluating, those responsible for reform can rely on vulnerability assessments that include the questions below.[48]

- Does any official position have excessive discretionary powers?
- What value is placed on the bribed services public officials could offer?
- What is the institution's budget? To what extent are there opportunities for embezzlement among the most important budget items?
- Does the institution have strong discretionary powers in determining its income, similar to the situation in tax authorities?
- How would one assess the organization's internal procedures with regard to corruption risks?
- Are there clear rules for the delegation and restriction of responsibilities?
- Are there clear recruitment rules?
- Is management obliged to carry out systematic checks?
- What are the rules of reporting?
- How would one assess the qualification and integrity of staff members?

- Do an official's duties include the awarding of contracts to outsiders? Are there guidelines for doing so? Is it easy to establish market prices?
- Are the institution's "customers" informed about their rights and the services they can expect?
- Do those who have suffered damages have the possibility to defend themselves?
- Are there signs of earlier corruption offenses?

Vulnerability assessments point out special risks, thus showing where it would be worthwhile to take a closer look. If research establishes who the victims of corruption are in the respective areas of civil service, it can be a starting point for gathering external information about the conduct of public officials.

In planning all measures, one has to consider that the respective public institution should continue functioning during the reform phase because its services are indispensable and because political backing for control policies would be lost if public institutions ceased to function while undergoing reform.

Improving Control Mechanisms in the Public Sector

Measures of corruption control in the public sector should be designed to influence the calculations of public officials, whom one assumes rationally weigh all advantages and disadvantages before deciding whether to act in a proper or in a corrupt manner. Essential variables to be considered in such calculations include the additional income that results from corrupt activities, the probability of being caught, the degree of punishment in case of exposure (including the loss of an official position), and the degree of difficulty with which corrupt agreements can be set up.[49]

The probability of uncovering corrupt conduct in the public sector rises with the clarity of responsibilities and the resulting likelihood of pinning corrupt behavior on an individual. If administrative procedures are tightened up, it is easier for those dependent on public services to localize the spot where an administrative process has been artificially delayed. The probability of uncovering corruption schemes increases when the discretionary powers of public officials are restricted. If there is little space for decisionmaking in the interpretation of guidelines, corrupt behavior is easier to pinpoint.

However, restrictions on discretionary powers can incur substantial costs because of a loss of flexibility in public services.

Attempts at raising the probability of revealing corruption schemes can also start with a look at how profits from corrupt conduct are used. One important point of access comprises information about the private living conditions of public officials. If their standard of living and their assets are not compatible with their legal income, there is justification for suspicion.[50] Hong Kong went so far with its successful corruption control campaign as to shift the burden of proof: A public service member must reveal his assets and prove that they stem from legal income.[51]

The public should be involved too. Independent complaint offices, which could possibly also take anonymous complaints, can be particularly helpful when corrupt public officials have overstepped the boundary to blackmail. If the public knows which services they can legitimately expect from a civil service office, individuals can then turn to a complaint office whenever their rightful services have not been fully provided as a consequence of misappropriation. One should not exclude the possibility of obtaining information from private individuals who have entered into a corruption contract with a public official. If the private individual in this case can reckon with a significantly lighter punishment than when caught without having informed the authorities, or if the private individual is granted impunity for acting as a principal witness in a successful case, then there is a chance of breaking the oath of silence that is part of a corruption contract.[52]

It is also essential to improve the systems that monitor public service.[53] Administrative procedures have to be designed in such a way that documents can only be manipulated with great difficulty. Cross-comparisons between connected administrative processes and random checks can raise the risk of discovery considerably. An investigation into completed administrative processes, even processes from the time prior to when the rules of the game were changed, back when officials hardly had to reckon with being discovered, can be useful in establishing what parts of an administrative body are plagued by corruption and who participates in it. The vulnerability assessments mentioned above can provide clues as to where such "backward-screening" might be particularly worthwhile.

All the above approaches to increasing the probability of revealing corruption share one core drawback: It is imperative that controlling bodies do not get involved in the network for distributing corrupt income and that those bodies cannot be bribed to conceal corrupt conduct. Such involvement creates a particularly grave problem in attempts to break up corruption rings based on strongly built groups.[54]

A further central variable in the calculations done by public officials is the severity of the punishment they have to face if they are caught. In an environment of systematic corruption, punishment is not necessarily a consequence of being caught. If illegal deals can be secured through bribery, then corruption offenses can be disregarded or explained away. Corrupt officials act in groups. After one group member is exposed, the other group members have, for reasons of self-defense, a vested interest in concealing information, disguising proof of corrupt conduct, and guaranteeing protection for the group member who was caught. The conditions for doing so are especially favorable if public officials from higher levels of the hierarchy are involved in the group. With the adoption of Western legal systems in developing countries, prosecution regulations have also been adopted, in part with more draconian penalties than Western industrial countries would allow. However, with regard to variables of punishment, the legally fixed severity of a penalty is not all that decisive. What plays a much bigger role is the question of whether, following exposure, penalties are actually imposed. The phrase "frying a few big fish" constitutes a basic rule in successful corruption control because that is the only way to change the expectation—developed during a phase of systematic corruption—that a conviction can be warded off by group members.[55]

Types of penalties can vary greatly. In addition to criminal sentencing or expulsion from the civil service, retirement income may be reduced or cancelled completely. The effectiveness of a penalty can be increased and have more influence on the calculations made by public officials if convicted officials are temporarily or permanently denied management positions in the private sector, thus creating significantly higher losses of income after removal from public service.[56] The power of a sentence or a dismissal can be further intensified by publishing news of the penalty and removing the title and creditworthiness of a convicted official.

Measures that make it difficult for officials to set up corruption-based relationships are also helpful. The search for potential partners in a corruption contract is linked to a certain risk of being caught, a risk that varies with the surrounding circumstances.[57] One approach to raising the price of information is the rotation of civil servants with the goal of cutting off well-greased relationships between active and passive partners in bribery or between civil servants who have direct contact with the public and those who allocate budgeted funds and their inspectors. Doubt is shed on the success of such a strategy when corrupt civil servants act in groups, and individual, newly rotated employees are quickly made privy to established rules. It is important to take precautions to impede repetitive corruption contracts, for example, by opening bidding procedures to new bidders. Obstacles to obtaining information will be higher for corrupt participants when the extent of corruption in the public sector decreases in general. It then becomes more difficult to find the necessary partners for corrupt conduct.

The costs and benefits of any corruption control policy have to be carefully weighed. There are not only direct costs, such as the salaries of additional officials entrusted with control duties. The costs of control policy include potential losses in efficiency that can occur when the work of public institutions becomes inflexible due to the introduction of rules aimed at restricting the discretionary powers of officials. Restrictions on civil rights are also a part of the price of corruption control and can occur when controlling authorities are granted far-reaching powers of investigation. The more far-reaching such powers are, the greater the chance of uncovering corrupt plots that are carried out by groups of officials with the involvement of supervisory bodies. At the same time, the danger of misuse increases because the government can purposely cut into the civil rights of its opponents or certain institutions of civil society, thus weakening the political power behind reform.

The reforms needed to curb corruption are primarily the responsibility of political bodies in developing countries. Hong Kong and Singapore were essentially able to ban corruption because the political elites in both countries were corruption-free. Corruption control measures could thus be carried out from top to bottom without any friction. Political will is a decisive resource in corruption control policy, and because political leaders are often involved in corrupt activities, political will constitutes a critical prerequisite.[58]

However, the reforms carried out in many developing countries in the past decades, reforms that have dismantled state-guaranteed monopolies and have led to democratization, could be pushed through despite the immediate interests of part of the administration and influential groups linked to them.[59] Even societies that suffer from epidemic corruption are not monolithic systems; even they have reform-oriented powers. Opportunities to control corruption can arise when there is a change in governments or in times of political crisis. Even without upheaval, the political will to reform can be created through a long-term process of changing awareness and mobilizing forces in civil society.[60]

Involving Civil Society

Civil society organizations and NGOs can play an important role in giving momentum to the reform process, especially when they form coalitions.[61] These coalitions may include citizens' groups, NGOs, religious organizations, trade unions, business associations, professional associations, academic organizations, the media, and so on.[62] A very important nucleus for civil society involvement are the national chapters of Transparency International, which today exist in more than 100 countries. Civil society organizations play an important role in exposing abuses of public authority, raising awareness about corruption issues, and strengthening the support of and the pressure from the public for an anticorruption policy.[63] They have succeeded in creating a growing understanding that fighting corruption is not an elite concern but a development issue. Beyond exposing abuses and raising awareness, civil society organizations have been engaged in more specific activities such as advocating legislative and regulatory change, improving procurement procedures, and improving monitoring. Civil society organizations work either in a more confrontational or a more collaborative way, depending on the focus of their work and whether there are partners for collaboration inside the government and its administrative bodies. In some countries (the Philippines, Indonesia, Peru) coalitions of civil society organizations succeeded in removing corrupt political leaders at the national and local levels.[64]

Coalitions of citizens' groups, religious groups, the press, and business groups are of the utmost importance in a situation of systemic corruption, where corrupt officials are protected by the president or people very close to him. Under such a condition, "normal" anticorruption policies, such as improving auditing systems, selecting public officials on the basis of competence, encouraging competition, or better defining the discretion of public officials, will have very limited success. A coalition of civil society organizations can attack systemic and organized corruption by disseminating information on the corrupt system, uncovering conspicuous consumption by those who have grown rich through corruption, and increasing political pressure for change.[65]

A special form of coalitions against corruption among government authorities, private companies, and civil society organizations are integrity pacts, which in many countries are facilitated or monitored by the national chapters of Transparency International. Integrity pacts are voluntary agreements underwritten by the parties directly involved in public procurement. They are designated to free businesses from the dilemma of having to bribe in order to be competitive in the bidding process.[66] The parties mutually agree not to request or to offer bribes—directly or through intermediaries—and to monitor this agreement. Legal sanctions against persons breaking the pact are decided in advance. For any violation by a bidder, sanctions may include denial or loss of contract, liability for damages to the authority inviting the public tender and to the competing bidders, and blacklisting for future biddings for an appropriate period of time. The publicity of the pact increases pressure on both sides to adhere to a transparent procurement procedure. Such integrity pacts can support a policy of containing corruption in public sector procurement processes. Of course, monitoring the obligations agreed upon in the pact is the key to success, and civil society organizations can play an important role in the monitoring process. Access to all relevant information is a must for successful monitoring; it includes information on design, selection of consultants, bidding documents, preselection of contractors, bidding procedures, bid evaluation, contracting, contract implementation, and supervision.[67] The pact depends on whistleblowers. Protection of whistleblowers is—as elsewhere in anticorruption policy—a critical issue.[68]

Anticorruption reform must be led from within the respective societies. National systems of integrity are essential to increasing the risks of and to lowering the returns expected from corruption. National systems of integrity are indispensable for success in making corruption a "high-risk" and "low-return" undertaking.[69] Anticorruption reform at the national level can be supported from the outside. If aid sponsors take their duties seriously, limit corruption in development cooperation, and secure transparency, they will at the same time support those people in developing countries who are committed to policies of corruption control.

Notes

1. The World Bank points to this problem (World Bank 1997a), pp. 56–57. Such risks are particularly prevalent in countries in which systematic corruption is linked to organized crime. In its guidelines, the World Bank provides its employees a twenty-four-hour hotline for advice on how to deal with cases of corruption. See Aguilar, Gill, and Pino (2000), pp. 49–50. See also World Bank (2005), p. 24, (2007a), p. 55.

2. This discrepancy is particularly large in the area of disaster relief, which gets much more attention in the media than general development aid.

3. German Federal Government (1997).

4. Richards (2003), p. 7.

5. Cooksey (2003), p. 3.

6. See company surveys for the *World Development Report 1997* or for the *Global Competitiveness Report 1996* and *1997* in Kaufmann and Wei (1999), pp. 6ff. Information on the sale of public offices in three Eastern European countries gathered from a survey of public officials can be found in Kaufmann, Pradhan, and Ryterman (1998), p. 4. See also Kaufmann (1998); World Bank (2002a), p. 22.

7. German Federal Government (1997).

8. In the wording of the German Anti-Corruption Clause, as part of bilateral government agreements (translation):

> The government of the Federal Republic of Germany and the government of . . . agree on their assessments of the negative consequences of corruption: it undermines good governance. It wastes precious financial means and has far-reaching negative effects on economic and social development. It jeopardizes the credibility of development cooperation and its public support and interferes with the efforts of all who are committed to fostering sustainable development. It impedes open and transparent competition based on price and quality. Both governments shall work together closely to guarantee transparency, accountability, and integrity in employing public funding. They shall cooperate in excluding any possible opportunities for corruption to arise in their development aid activities.

Letter of September 26, 1997, from the Federal Ministry of Economic Cooperation and Development to the author. See also Bundesministerium für wirtschaftliche Zusammenarbeit und Entwicklung (2002), pp. 8–9.

9. World Bank (undated).

10. Stückelberger (2003), p. 21, referring to an internal study of the Swiss Agency for Development and Cooperation on the efficiency of different instruments to combat corruption, including the anticorruption clause.

11. On the following, see World Bank (1997a), pp. 29ff; World Bank (undated).

12. World Bank (2000), p. 68.

13. The timing of payment can also be an important indicator. If bribe money is paid in advance, an agent has to insist on high advance payments from his client. See Lambsdorff (1997), p. 11, fn. 31.

14. Wiehen (2001), pp. 90–92.

15. See World Bank Resident Staff, Indonesia (1998).

16. Guidelines for Procurement under IBRD Loans and IDA Credits, para. 1.15. See World Bank (undated).

17. World Bank (2000), pp. 17–18; World Bank (2005), pp. 17ff; Thornburgh (2004), pp. 2, 7.

18. See World Bank (2008).

19. World Bank (2008), pp. 42ff.

20. Thornburgh, Gainer, and Walker (2002), pp. 75ff.

21. Moran, Pope, and Doig (2004), p. 57.

22. See the recommendations for debarment policies in ibid., pp. 23ff.

23. See also Clarke (2001), pp. 108, 112.

24. World Bank (1997a), p. 46, fn. 43.

25. Wade (1985), p. 478, points to this problem in his case studies on India.

26. This has been proposed, for instance, by the group of World Bank employees who took a stance on corruption in World Bank projects in Indonesia. See World Bank Resident Staff, Indonesia (1998).

27. See Caritas Internationalis (1999) for one attempt at establishing such basic rules within an international network of organizations. M. Kandasami (1997) provides a complete overview of rules for securing transparency within NGOs, using India as an example.

28. German Federal Government (1997), p. 4.

29. Celarier (1996) and Lewis (1997) cited by Johnson (1998), p. 14.

30. Johnson (1998), pp. 18–19.

31. A recent example of such a partial approach: In 2007, the World Bank withdrew US$33 million as part of a large road construction program loan in the Philippines due to "strong signs of collusion and excessive pricing" in the bidding process for two contracts. See Agence France Presse (2007).

32. World Bank (2006), pp. 9, 11.

33. World Bank (1997a), p. 7.

34. On this shifting of funds, see Hemmer (1988), pp. 746–747, 790–791; Wolff (2005), pp. 261ff.

35. Anger (2004), p. 48.

36. For an example of failed corruption control policy in a strictly regulated agricultural market, see the case study about an anonymously presented

developing African country in Klitgaard (1998), pp. 156ff. Klitgaard traces the failure of control efforts to flaws in implementation that are actually presented in this example. However, the wide gaps between state-set buying prices and the black market created strong incentives for bribery. In addition, consumer prices were so heavily subsidized that smuggling foodstuffs into neighboring countries made an extremely lucrative business. Under such conditions, even a more effectively enforced control policy would fail if it had no power to change agricultural policy.

37. Bailey (2003), p. 20.

38. See Streissler (1981), p. 303: "All forms of corruption thus result from what the economist would call market limitations or market imperfections. . . . An entrepreneurial market economy can only ever be a component of the organization of our society. . . . Our society is only bearable because there is—thank heavens!—no perfect market for homicide activities!"

39. See Goudie and Stasavage (1997), pp. 21–22; Kaufmann (1997a); Wiehen (2003).

40. A study on the acceptance of corruption control measures based on a survey taken among public officials in Australia (New South Wales) points to factors that impede support of such measures by civil servants. One of those factors is the conviction that corrupt behavior can be justified under certain circumstances. See Pope (2000), Chap. 2.

41. Bailey (2003), pp. 27–28.

42. On reforms in the Philippine tax administration, started after corruption had led to drastic decreases in tax income, see Klitgaard (1988), pp. 52ff, especially 60–61. Reform success was not sustainable because President Marcos was not willing to do without his cronies in tax administration positions, whereby one can suspect a certain connection to the financing of his last campaign.

43. Cremer (1995), p. 223.

44. The success of controls on previously systematic corruption in the police force of Hong Kong is mainly attributed to the institutional independence of a controlling body newly founded in 1973 (Independent Commission Against Corruption). See Klitgaard (1988), pp. 107, 115. On the rights of the ICAC, see ICAC Review Committee (1996).

45. Bailey (2003), p. 30; Pope and Vogl (2000).

46. For the following, see Klitgaard (1988) and his case studies on policies of corruption control in the Philippines, Hong Kong, and Singapore; Klitgaard (1998); Klitgaard (2000).

47. Klitgaard (1988), p. 49.

48. On this topic, see Klitgaard (1988), pp. 84–85, based on the Internal Control Guidelines of the Office of Management and Budget, Washington, DC.

49. On the calculations done by potentially corrupt actors, see, for example, Neugebauer (1978), pp. 14–64; Pritzl (1997), pp. 81–133; Borner and Schwyzer (1999), pp. 21ff.

50. Colombo (1997), para. 5ff.

51. Klitgaard (1988), pp. 104–105.

52. On this topic, see Lambsdorff (1997), pp. 13ff. On the issue of impunity within the context of combating corruption, see Feneley (1997).

53. See Garamfalvi (1997) and the Philippine case study in Klitgaard (1988), pp. 52ff.

54. In the attempt at limiting corruption in the Philippine tax administration, members of the secret service were employed as coworkers and placed in the tax administration to overcome strong group structures. The independent controlling authority in Hong Kong recruited officers from Great Britain for the same purpose. See Klitgaard (1988), pp. 53, 110.

55. Klitgaard (1998), p. 4.

56. Providing information to potential private sector employers about the reasons behind dismissals has been part of corruption control policy in Singapore. See Klitgaard (1988), p. 129.

57. If a "culture of ambiguity" has been established in the relationship between civil servants and the public, it allows for investigations into the willingness of a partner to participate in corrupt business dealings without making it clear from the start that such investigations may become relevant in a criminal case.

58. See Kpundeh (1998).

59. Klitgaard (1998).

60. Gray and Kaufmann (1998), p. 9.

61. As overview, see Eigen (2004), pp. 12ff.

62. For examples of the involvement of religious organizations, see Stückelberger (2003).

63. Transparency International (2003), "Corruption Fighters' Tool Kit," 2002–2003, Section I. CD-ROM.

64. Bailey (2003), pp. 34ff.

65. Klitgaard (2000).

66. Eigen (2004), pp. 17–18.

67. Transparency International (2002), pp. 3ff.

68. Bailey (2003), pp. 39–40.

69. Eigen (2004), pp. 19–20.

Bibliography

Agence France Presse (2007). "Philippine Government to Address World Bank Corruption Claims." November 19, 2007. http://afp.google.com/article/ALeqM5hIpD7yWxEYRmf0fp6ykIYO6fYmBw (02.01.2008).

Aguilar, Mario A., Jit B. S. Gill, and Livio Pino (2000). *Preventing Fraud and Corruption in World Bank Projects: A Guide for Staff.* Washington, DC: World Bank.

Aicher, Josef (1981). "Korruptionsfördernde und korruptionshemmende Bedingungen bei der Vergabe öffentlicher Aufträge: Überlegungen und Alternativen zur Reform des Vergaberechtes." In Christian Brünner, ed., *Korruption und Kontrolle.* Wien: Böhlau, pp. 349–433.

Alam, M. Shahid (1989). "Anatomy of Corruption: An Approach to the Political Economy of Underdevelopment." *American Journal of Economics and Sociology* 48, no. 4, October, pp. 441–456.

Alam, M. Shahid (1990). "Some Economic Costs of Corruption in LDCs." *Journal of Development Studies* 27, no. 1, October, pp. 89–97.

Anderson, James H., and Cheryl W. Gray (2006). *Anticorruption in Transition 3: Who Is Succeeding . . . and Why?* Washington, DC: World Bank. http://siteresources.worldbank.org/INTECA/Resources/ACT3.pdf (03.01.2008).

Anderson, Mary B. (1999). *Do No Harm: How Aid Can Support Peace—or War.* Boulder: Lynne Rienner.

Anderson, Mary B., ed. (2000). *Options for Aid in Conflict: Lessons from Field Experience.* Cambridge, MA: Collaborative for Development Action.

Anger, Joakim (2004). "Anti-corruption Strategies in Development Cooperation." Swedish International Development Cooperation Agency. Corruption Working Paper No. 3.

Articus, Stephan (1990). "Sozialpolitik in Entwicklungsländern: Darstellung und Analysen Sozialer Sicherung in Afrika, Asien und Lateinamerika." Deutscher Verein für öffentliche und private Fürsorge. Reihe Dissertationen, Diplomarbeiten, Dokumente No. 17. Frankfurt am Main: Deutscher Verein.

Bailey, Bruce (2003). *Synthesis of Lessons Learned of Donor Practices in Fighting Corruption.* OECD, Development Assistance Committee Network on Governance. DCD/DAC/GOVNET(2003)1. June 23, 2003 (unclassified). http://www.oecd.org/dataoecd/14/44/19936969.pdf (03.01.2008).

Bales, Sarah, and Martin Rama (2002). "Are Public Sector Workers Underpaid? Appropriate Comparators in a Development Country." World Bank Policy Research Working Paper No. 2747. Washington, DC: World Bank.

Bapna, Manish (2004). Testimony Before the US Senate Committee on Foreign Relations Hearing, *Combating Corruption in the Multilateral Development Banks.* May 13, 2004. http://www.foreign.senate.gov/hearings/2004/hrg040513a.html (03.01.2008).

Bardhan, Pranab (1997). "Corruption and Development: A Review of Issues." *Journal of Economic Literature* 35, September, pp. 1320–1346.

Bastøe, Per Øyvind, Mette Masst (2001). "How to Prevent Corruption in Development Aid-Funded Projects and Programs." In Lara M. Gabriel and Rick Stapenhurst, with Mary Thomas, eds., *The Role of Bilateral Donors in Fighting Corruption.* Washington, DC: World Bank, pp. 71–77.

Bierbrauer, Günter (1979). "Kognitive Theorien in der Sozialpsychologie." In Anneliese Heigl-Evers and Ulrich Streeck, eds., *Lewin und die Folgen: Sozialpsychologie, Gruppendynamik, Gruppentherapie.* Die Psychologie des 20. Jahrhunderts. Band VIII. Zürich: Kindler, pp. 86–97.

BMZ (Bundesministerium für wirtschaftliche Zusammenarbeit und Entwicklung) (2002). "Korruptionsbekämpfung." BMZ-spezial No. 045. Bonn. June. http://www.bmz.de/de/service/infothek/fach/spezial/spezial045pdf.pdf (05.01.2008).

BMZ (Bundesministerium für wirtschaftliche Zusammenarbeit und Entwicklung) (2007). "Entwicklungsorientierte Transformation bei fragiler Staatlichkeit und schlechter Regierungsführung." BMZ Konzepte 149. Berlin. March. http://www.bmz.de/de/service/infothek/fach/konzepte/konzept149.pdf (03.01.2008).

Borner, Silvio, and Christophe Schwyzer (1999). "Die Bekämpfung der Bestechung im Lichte der Neuen Politischen Ökonomie." In Mark Pieth and Peter Eigen, eds., *Korruption im internationalen Geschäftsverkehr. Bestandsaufnahme, Bekämpfung, Prävention.* Neuwied: Luchterhand, pp. 17–39.

Bosshard, Peter (1998). "Sieben Milliarden Dollar für die Korruption? Die Korruption in Indonesien, die Weltbank, und die Schweiz." Manuscript. Declaration of Bern, September 22, 1998.

Braun, Gerald (1988). "Die hilflose Überlegenheit des Experten." *Vierteljahresberichte: Probleme der internationalen Zusammenarbeit.* Friedrich Ebert Stiftung. No. 114. December, pp. 349–358.

Camerer, Lala (2001). "Terms of Engagement for Bilateral Donors: A South African Perspective from Civil Society." In Lara M. Gabriel and Rick Stapenhurst, with Mary Thomas, eds., *The Role of Bilateral Donors in Fighting Corruption.* Washington, DC: World Bank, pp. 181–200.

Caritas Internationalis (1999). *Common Financial Standards for Project Management.* General Assembly of Caritas Internationalis, Rome, June.

Cassen, Robert, et al. (1986). *Does Aid Work? Report to an Intergovernmental Task Force.* Oxford: Clarendon.

Caufield, Catherine (1997). *Masters of Illusion: The World Bank and the Poverty of Nations.* London: Macmillan.

Celarier, Michelle (1996). "Stealing the Family Silver." *Euromoney,* February, pp. 62–66.

Clarke, Jeremy (2001). "Improving Coordination of Anti-Corruption Policies and Activities by Donor Agencies." In Lara M. Gabriel and Rick Stapenhurst, with Mary Thomas, eds., *The Role of Bilateral Donors in Fighting Corruption.* Washington, DC: World Bank, pp. 97–113.

Colombo, Gherardo (1997). "Monitoring the Assets and Lifestyles of Public Decision-Makers. Can It Be Made to Work?" Paper presented at the 8th International Anti-Corruption Conference, Lima, Peru, September 7–11.

Cooksey, Brian (2003). "Aid and Corruption. A Worm's-Eye View of Donor Policies and Practices." Paper presented at the 11th International Anti-Corruption Conference, Seoul, South Korea,

May 26–29. Workshop no. 5.6: Corruption and Donor Policies and Practices.

Court of Auditors (2000). "Special Report No. 4/2000 on Rehabilitation Actions for ACP Countries as an Instrument to Prepare for Normal Development Aid, Accompanied by the Commission's Replies" (2000/C 113/01). *Official Journal of the European Communities.* April 19, 2000. http://eur-lex.europa.eu/LexUriServ/site/en/oj/2000/c_113/c_11320000419en00010032.pdf (03.01.2008).

Cremer, Georg (1990). "Schein-Consulting, Titelblattgeschäfte, Kick-back—Auftragsforschung als Instrument der Mittelumlenkung: Beobachtungen zum Wissenschaftssektor in Indonesien." *Internationales Asienforum/International Quarterly for Asian Studies* 21, Nos. 3–4, pp. 209–234.

Cremer, Georg (1995). *Suchverhalten, Statuserwartungen und offene Arbeitslosigkeit in Entwicklungsökonomien mit rasch expandierendem Bildungssystem: Eine Untersuchung am Beispiel Indonesiens.* Volkswirtschaftliche Schriften No. 445. Berlin: Duncker and Humblot.

Cremer, Georg (1996). "'Das kommt ja sowieso nicht an!' Zum Problem des Mißbrauchs in der Katastrophenhilfe." In Rolf Hanisch and Peter Moßmann, eds., *Katastrophen und ihre Bewältigung in den Ländern des Südens.* Schriften des Deutschen Übersee-Instituts Hamburg, No. 33, pp. 163–182.

Cremer, Georg (1997). "Verlängert Nothilfe Kriege?" In Deutscher Caritasverband, ed., *Caritas '98.* Jahrbuch des Deutschen Caritasverbandes. Freiburg: Deutscher Caritasverband, pp. 195–205.

Cremer, Georg (1998a). "Korruption und Korruptionskontrolle in der Entwicklungszusammenarbeit." *Verfassung und Recht in Übersee* 31, no. 1, pp. 6–23.

Cremer, Georg (1998b). "On the Problem of Misuse in Emergency Aid." *Journal of Humanitarian Assistance.* University of Cambridge. http://www.jha.ac/articles/a042.htm, posted June 15 (03.01.2008).

Cremer, Georg (2002). "The Challenge of Partner-Oriented Emergency Aid." In Institut für Friedenssicherung und Humanitäres Völkerrecht, ed., *Europe and Humanitarian Aid—What Future?—Learning from Crises.* Bochum: European University Press, pp. 189–195.

Cremer, Georg (2004). "Entwicklungszusammenarbeit: Begrenzung der Korruption durch Abbau von Informationssperren." *Vierteljahresberichte zur Wirtschaftsforschung* 73, no. 2, pp. 318–329.

DFID (Department for International Development) (1999/2002). "Anti-Corruption Strategy for DFID." Paper 3A. Document undersigned by Governance Department, December 10, 1999. Additional date stated: September 30, 2002. http://www.u4.no/document/showdoc.cfm?id=8 (03.01.2008).

de Soto, Hernando (1992). *Marktwirtschaft von unten: Die unsichtbare Revolution in Entwicklungsländern.* Zürich: Orell Füssli Verlag.

De Speville, Bertrand (1997). *Hong Kong: Policy Initiatives Against Corruption.* Development Centre Studies. Paris: OECD.

Devine, Vera (2005). "Corruption in Post-War Reconstruction: The Experience of Bosnia and Herzegovina." In Daniel Large, ed., *Corruption in Post-War Reconstruction: Confronting the Vicious Circle.* Beirut: Technopress, pp. 81–96.

DEZA (Direktion für Entwicklung und Zusammenarbeit, Swiss) (1998). *Korruptionsbekämpfung. Leitlinien.* Bern: DEZA.

Dixit, Kunda (1995). "Fighting Corruption in the Aid Business." *Third World Resurgence* (Penang) 60, pp. 15–17.

Duffield, Mark (1994). "The Political Economy of Internal War: Asset Transfer, Complex Emergencies, and International Aid." In Joanna Macrae and Anthony Zwi, eds., *War and Hunger: Rethinking International Responses to Complex Emergencies.* London: Zed, pp. 50–69.

Eigen, Peter (2004). "Chasing Corruption Around the World: How Civil Society Strengthens Global Governance." Arthur and Frank Payne Distinguished Lecture, Stanford Institute for International Studies, October 4. http://iis-db.stanford.edu/evnts/3922/Eigen10'04.pdf (05.01.2008).

Feneley, John (1997). "Witness Protection Schemes: Pitfalls, Best Practice, Covert Investigations." Paper presented at the 8th International Anti-Corruption Conference, Lima, Peru, September 7–11.

Festinger, Leon (1957). *A Theory of Cognitive Dissonance.* Stanford: Stanford University Press.

Festinger, Leon (1978). *Theorie der kognitiven Dissonanz.* Bern: Huber.

Fleck, Christian, and Helmut Kuzmics (1985). *Korruption: Zur*

Soziologie nicht immer abweichenden Verhaltens. Königstein: Athenäum.

Frey, René L. (1978). "Infrastruktur." In *Handwörterbuch der Wirtschaftswissenschaft*, vol. 4. Stuttgart, Tübingen, Göttingen: Fischer, Mohr, Vandenhoeck u. Ruprecht, pp. 200–215.

Furubotn, Eirik, and Rudolf Richter (2005). *Institutions and Economic Theory: The Contribution of the New Institutional Economics*. 2nd ed. Ann Arbor: University of Michigan Press.

Galtung, Fredrik (2005). "Introduction: The Corruption Dimension of Post-War Reconstruction." In Daniel Large, ed., *Corruption in Post-War Reconstruction: Confronting the Vicious Circle*. Beirut: Technopress, pp. 18–31.

Garamfalvi, L. (1997). "Corruption in the Public Expenditures Management Process." Paper presented at the 8th International Anti-Corruption Conference, Lima, Peru, September 7–11.

German Federal Government (1994). Antwort der Bundesregierung auf die große Anfrage der Abgeordneten Rudolf Binding, Evelyn Fischer (Gräfenheinchen), Monika Gansefort, weiterer Abgeordneter und der Fraktion der SPD: Humanitäres Spendenwesen in der Bundesrepublik—Schwerpunkt Auslandshilfe. Deutscher Bundestag. Drucksache 12/8248, July 7.

German Federal Government (1997). Antwort der Bundesregierung auf die Kleine Anfrage der Abgeordneten Dr. Ingomar Hauchler, Brigitte Adler u.a.: Umsetzung der Beschlüsse der Organisation für wirtschaftliche Zusammenarbeit und Entwicklung zur Korruptionsbekämpfung in der Entwicklungszusammenarbeit. Deutscher Bundestag. Drucksache 13/8277, July 17.

Ginneken, Wouter van (2003). "Extending Social Security: Policies for Developing Countries." Extension of Social Security Paper No. 13. Geneva: International Labour Organization, Social Security Policy and Development Branch. http://www.ilo.org/wcmsp5/groups/public/---dgreports/---dcomm/documents/publication/kd00061.pdf (04.01.2008).

Goudie, Andrew W., and David Stasavage (1997). "Corruption: The Issues." OECD Development Centre, Technical Paper No. 122. http://www.oecd.org/dataoecd/29/59/1849511.pdf. (06.01.2008).

Gould, David J. (1979). "The Problem of Seepage in International Development Assistance: Why United States Aid to Zaire Goes Astray." *Civilisations* (Brussels) 29, nos. 3–4, pp. 253–267.

Gransow, Bettina (1991). "Die Gabe und die Korruption: Form- und

Funktionswandel des Tausches in China." *Internationales Asienforum/International Quarterly for Asian Studies* 22, nos. 3–4, pp. 343–360.

Gray, Cheryl W., and Daniel Kaufmann (1998). "Corruption and Development." *Finance and Development* 35, no. 1, March, pp. 7–10.

Gray, Clive (1979). "Civil Service Compensation in Indonesia." *Bulletin of Indonesian Economic Studies* (Australian National University) 15, no. 1, March, pp. 85–113.

Grødeland, Åse B., Tatyana Y. Koshechkina, and William L. Miller (1998). "'Foolish to Give and More Foolish Not to Take': In-depth Interviews with Post-Communist Citizens on Their Everyday Use of Bribes and Contacts." *Europe-Asia Studies* 50, no. 4, pp. 651–677.

Gupta, Sanjeev, Hamid Davoodi, and Erwin Tiongson (2000). "Corruption and the Provision of Health Care and Education Services." Working Paper WP/00/116. Washington, DC: IMF. http://www.imf.org/external/pubs/ft/wp/2000/wp00116.pdf (05.01.2008).

Hadisumarto, Djunaedi (1974). "The Indonesian Civil Service and Its Reform Movements." Ph.D. diss., University of Southern California.

Heidenheimer, Arnold J., Michael Johnston, and Victor T. Le Vine, eds. (1999). *Political Corruption. A Handbook.* 5th printing. New Brunswick: Transaction.

Hemmer, Hans-Rimbert (1988). *Wirtschaftsprobleme der Entwicklungsländer.* 2nd ed. München: Vahlen.

Holdmann, Tim (1997). "Korruption und Technische Zusammenarbeit." Studienarbeit. Betreuer Heiko Körner. Technische Universität Darmstadt. Fachgebiet Wirtschaftspolitik. Fachbereich 1—Rechts—und Wirtschaftswissenschaften. September. Darmstadt: Selbstverlag.

Huntington, Samuel P. (1968/1999). "Modernization and Corruption." In Arnold J. Heidenheimer, Michael Johnston, and Victor T. Le Vine, eds., *Political Corruption: A Handbook.* 5th printing. New Brunswick: Transaction, pp. 377–388. First published in Huntington, *Political Order in Changing Societies,* New Haven: Yale University Press, pp. 59–71.

ICAC Review Committee. Corruption Prevention Department (1996). "Note on the Corruption Prevention Department (Hong Kong

ICAC)." In Jeremy Pope, ed., *National Integrity Systems: The TI [Transparency International] Source Book.* Berlin: Transparency International, Part C: G5.

Internet Center for Corruption Research (1997). "1997 Corruption Perception Index." A joint initiative of the University of Passau and Transparency International. http://www.icgg.org/corruption.cpi_olderindices_1997.html (04.01.2008).

Internet Center for Corruption Research (2006). "2006 Corruption Perception Index." A joint initiative of the University of Passau and Transparency International. http://www.icgg.org/corruption.cpi_2006_data.html (04.01.2008).

Jessen, Brigitte (1994). "Fremdhilfe und die Mobilisierung interner Ressourcen dargestellt am Beispiel der NGO-Arbeit in Bangladesch und Thailand." In Rolf Hanisch and Rodger Wegner, eds., *Nichtregierungsorganisationen und Entwicklung: Auf dem Weg zu mehr Realismus.* Schriften des Deutschen Übersee Instituts Hamburg, No. 28, pp. 45–68.

Johnson, Ben (1998). *The World Bank's Anti-Corruption Policy: A Description and Analysis.* St. Louis: Washington University. Manuscript.

Kaiser, Günther (1991). "Korruption aus Sicht des internationalen Wirtschaftsrechts." In *Korruption: Eine Herausforderung für Gesellschaft und Kirche.* Bad Boll: Evangelische Akademie. Protokolldienst 8/91, pp. 25–40.

Kandasami, M. (1997). *Governance and Financial Management in Non-Profit Organisations: A Reference Manual.* Rev. ed. New Delhi: Caritas India.

Kaufmann, Daniel (1997a). "Economic Corruption. Some Facts." Paper presented at the 8th International Anti-Corruption Conference, Lima, Peru, September 7–11.

Kaufmann, Daniel (1997b). "Why Is Ukraine's Economy—and Russia's—Not Growing?" *Transition,* April, pp. 5–8.

Kaufmann, Daniel (1998). "Challenges in the Next Stage of Anti-corruption." September. http://www.worldbank.org/wbi/governance/pdf/challenges.pdf (27.03.2008).

Kaufmann, Daniel (2004). "Corruption, Governance, and Security: Challenges for the Rich Countries and the World." http://ssrn.com/abstract=605801 (05.01.2008).

Kaufmann, Daniel, Aart Kraay, and Massimo Mastruzzi (2003). "Governance Matters III: Governance Indicators for 1996–2002."

World Bank. Working Paper (draft for comment). http://papers.ssrn.com/sol3/papers.cfm?abstract_id=405841 (05.01.2008).

Kaufmann, Daniel, Aart Kraay, and Pablo Zoido-Lobatón (1999). "Governance Matters." Policy Research Working Paper No. 2196. Washington, DC: World Bank Development Research Group.

Kaufmann, Daniel, Sanjay Pradhan, and Randi Ryterman (1998). "New Frontiers in Diagnosing and Combating Corruption." World Bank, Development Economics Vice Presidency and Poverty Reduction and Economic Management Network, No. 7, October. http://www1.worldbank.org/prem/PREMNotes/premnote7.pdf (05.01.2008).

Kaufmann, Daniel, and Shang-Jin Wei (1999). "Does 'Grease Money' Speed Up the Wheels of Commerce?" World Bank Research Working Paper 2254. http://papers.ssrn.com/sol3/papers.cfm?abstract_id=629191 (05.01.2008).

Klaveren, Jacob van (1957). "Die historische Erscheinung der Korruption, in ihrem Zusammenhang mit der Staats- und Gesellschaftsstruktur betrachtet." *Vierteljahresschrift für Sozial- und Wirtschaftsgeschichte.* Band 44, pp. 289–324.

Klitgaard, Robert (1988). *Controlling Corruption.* Berkeley: University of California Press.

Klitgaard, Robert (1998). "International Cooperation Against Corruption." *Finance and Development* 35, no. 1, March, pp. 3–6.

Klitgaard, Robert (2000). "Subverting Corruption." *Finance and Development* 27, no. 2, June.

Kpundeh, Sahr J. (1998). "Political Will: The Core of Anti-Corruption Reforms." Paper presented at the conference "National and International Approaches to Improving Integrity and Transparency in Government." Organized by the Organization for Economic Co-operation and Development and the Organization for Security and Co-operation in Europe, with the support of the Economic Development Institute of the World Bank. Paris, July 15–16.

Kpundeh, Sahr J. (2001). "Procedures and Guidelines of Donor Agencies to Prevent and Suppress Corruption." In Lara M. Gabriel and Rick Stapenhurst, with Mary Thomas, eds., *The Role of Bilateral Donors in Fighting Corruption.* Washington, DC: World Bank, pp. 55–70.

Kramer, John M. (1977/1999). "Political Corruption in the USSR." In Arnold J. Heidenheimer, Michael Johnston, and Victor T. Le Vine, eds., *Political Corruption: A Handbook.* 5th printing. New

Brunswick: Transaction, pp. 449–465. First published in *Western Political Quarterly* 30, no. 2, June 1977, pp. 213–224.

Kreppel, Thomas (1995). "Zur steuerrechtlichen Behandlung von deutschem Korruptionsaufwand in Entwicklungsländern." In Uwe Holtz and Manfred Kulessa, eds., *Korruption als Entwicklungshindernis.* Part 1, *Läßt sich Korruption durch rechtliche Maßnahmen in Deutschland unterbinden?* Materialien der Gemeinsamen Konferenz Kirche und Entwicklung (GKKE) zum Dialogprogramm D11. Bonn: GKKE.

Kurer, Oskar (2003). "Was ist Korruption? Der Stand der Diskussion um eine Definition von Korruption." In Oskar Kurer, ed., *Korruption und Governance aus interdisziplinärer Sicht.* Neustadt an der Aisch: Degener, pp. 41–51.

Lambsdorff, Johann Graf (1997). "Transaktionskosten der Korruption: Eine institutionenökonomische Betrachtung." Diskussionsbeiträge aus dem Volkswirtschaftlichen Seminar der Universität Göttingen No. 94. December.

Lambsdorff, Johann Graf (1999a). "Wie kann man Korruption messen? Der Korruptionsindex von Transparency International." *Entwicklung und Zusammenarbeit* 40, no. 11, pp. 300–303.

Lambsdorff, Johann Graf (1999b). "Korruption als mühseliges Geschäft: Eine Transaktionskostenanalyse." In Mark Pieth and Peter Eigen, eds., *Korruption im internationalen Geschäftsverkehr. Bestandsaufnahme, Bekämpfung, Prävention.* Neuwied: Luchterhand, pp. 56–87.

Lambsdorff, Johann Graf (2001). "How Corruption in Government Affects Public Welfare: A Review of Theories." Discussion Paper No. 9. University of Göttingen, Center for Globalization and Europeanization of the Economy.

Lambsdorff, Johann Graf (2002). "What Nurtures Corrupt Deals? On the Role of Confidence and Transaction Costs." In Donatella Della Porta and Susan Rose-Ackerman, eds., *Corrupt Exchanges: Empirical Themes in the Politics and Political Economy of Corruption.* Baden-Baden: Nomos.

Lambsdorff, Johann Graf, and Sitki Utku Teksoz (2005). "Corrupt Relational Contracting." In Johann Graf Lambsdorff, Markus Taube, and Matthias Schramm, eds., *The New Institutional Economics of Corruption.* London: Routledge, pp. 138–151.

Langerbein, Heinrich (2000). "In der internationalen

Entwicklungszusammenarbeit stecken erhebliche Finanzreserven." *Aus Politik und Zeitgeschichte*. B9/2000, pp. 32–38.

Leff, Nathaniel H. (1964/1999). "Economic Development Through Bureaucratic Corruption." In Arnold J. Heidenheimer, Michael Johnston, and Victor T. Le Vine, eds. (1999), *Political Corruption: A Handbook*. 5th printing. New Brunswick: Transaction, pp. 389–403. First published in *American Behavioral Scientist* 8, no. 3, November 1964, pp. 8–14.

Leisinger, Klaus M. (1997). *Unternehmensethik: Globale Verantwortung und modernes Management*. München: Beck.

Lewis, Paul (1997). "2 Global Lenders Use Leverage to Combat Corruption." *New York Times*, August 4, p. A4.

Lugar, Richard (2004). Opening statement before the US Senate Committee on Foreign Relations hearing, *Combating Corruption in the Multilateral Development Banks*. May 13. http://www.foreign.senate.gov/hearings/2004/hrg040513a.html (05.01.2008).

Lui, Francis T. (1985). "An Equilibrium Queuing Model of Bribery." *Journal of Political Economy* 93, no. 4, August, pp. 760–781.

MacAndrews, Colin (1986). "The Structure of Government in Indonesia." In Colin MacAndrews, ed., *Central Government and Local Development in Indonesia*. Singapore: Oxford University Press, pp. 20–41.

Marschdorf, Hans Joachim (1999). "Möglichkeiten der Feststellung und Prävention von Bestechungsleistungen aus Sicht des Bestechenden." In Mark Pieth and Peter Eigen, eds., *Korruption im internationalen Geschäftsverkehr. Bestandsaufnahme, Bekämpfung, Prävention*. Neuwied: Luchterhand, pp. 423–447.

Mauro, Paolo (1996). "The Effects of Corruption on Growth, Investment, and Government Expenditure." Working Paper 96/98. Washington, DC: International Monetary Fund.

Mauro, Paolo (1997). "Why Worry About Corruption?" Economic Issues No. 6. Washington, DC: International Monetary Fund.

Moran, Jon, Jeremy Pope, and Alain Doig (2004). "Debarment as an Anti-Corruption Means: A Review Report." Utstein Anti-Corruption Resource Centre. September. http://www.u4.no/themes/debarment/debarmentreport.pdf (05.01.2008).

Myrdal, Gunnar (1968). *Asian Drama: An Inquiry into the Poverty of Nations*. Vol. 2. New York: Pantheon.

Neugebauer, Gregory (1978). *Grundzüge einer ökonomischen Theorie der Korruption: Eine Studie über Bestechung.* Basler sozialökonomische Studien, vol. 9. Basel: Schulthess.

NORAD (Norwegian Agency for Development Cooperation) (2000). "NORAD's Good Governance and Anti-Corruption Action Plan 2000–2001." NORAD Report 2000/1. February 29. http://www.norad.no/norsk/files/HandlingsplanKorrEngeksl.doc (05.01.2008).

Nye, Joseph S. (1967/1999). "Corruption and Political Development: A Cost-Benefit Analysis." In Arnold J. Heidenheimer, Michael Johnston, and Victor T. Le Vine, eds. (1999). *Political Corruption. A Handbook.* 5th printing. New Brunswick: Transaction, pp. 963–983. First published in *American Political Science Review* 61, no. 2, June 1967, pp. 417–427.

OECD (Organization for Economic Cooperation and Development) (1993). "Development Co-operation." Development Assistance Committee Report. Paris: OECD.

OECD (2000). *No Longer Business as Usual: Fighting Bribery and Corruption.* Paris: OECD.

Osborne, Denis (1993). "Action for Better Government: A Role for Donors." *IDS Bulletin* (Brighton) 24, no. 1, pp. 67–73.

Palmier, Leslie (1985). *The Control of Bureaucratic Corruption: Case Studies in Asia.* Delhi: Allied Publishers.

Pieth, Mark (1999). "Die Strafbarkeit der aktiven Bestechung ausländischer Beamter." In Mark Pieth and Peter Eigen, eds., *Korruption im internationalen Geschäftsverkehr: Bestandsaufnahme, Bekämpfung, Prävention.* Neuwied: Luchterhand, pp. 341–353.

Pope, Jeremy, ed. (2000). *National Integrity Systems. The TI [Transparency International] Source Book.* Berlin: Transparency International. http://www.transparency.org/publications/sourcebook (05.01.2008).

Pope, Jeremy, and Frank Vogl (2000). "Making Anti-corruption Agencies More Effective." *Finance and Development* 27, no. 2, June. http://www.imf.org/external/pubs/ft/fandd/2000/06/pope.htm (05.01.2008).

Pritzl, Rupert F. J. (1997). *Korruption und Rent-Seeking in Lateinamerika: Zur politischen Ökonomie autoritärer politischer Systeme.* Baden-Baden: Nomos.

Quah, Jon S. T. (1999). "Singapore's Experience in Curbing Corruption." In Arnold J. Heidenheimer, Michael Johnston, and Victor T. Le Vine, eds. (1999), *Political Corruption. A Handbook.* 5th printing. New Brunswick: Transaction, pp. 841–853.

RDCMD (Research and Documentation Centre for Manpower and Development) (1988). "Labour in the Public Service: Indonesian Report." Jakarta: RDCMD.

Reinikka, Ritva, and Nathanael Smith (2004). *Public Expenditure Tracking Surveys in Education. International Institute for Educational Planning.* Paris: UNESCO. http://www.unesco.org/iiep/PDF/pubs/Reinikka.pdf (27.03.2008).

Reinikka, Ritva, and Jakob Svensson (2002). "Measuring and Understanding Corruption at the Micro Level." Working Document. http://www1.worldbank.org/publicsector/anticorrupt/corruptionBielefledl1.doc (05.01.2008).

Reinikka, Ritva, and Jakob Svensson (2006). "Using Micro Surveys to Measure and Explain Corruption." *World Development* 34, no. 2, pp. 359–370. http://www1.worldbank.org/publicsector/anticorrupt/feb06course/world%20Development%20article%20Feb%202006.pdf (27.03.2008).

Richards, Kathy (2003). "Facing the Challenge of Civil Society Representation: Donor Governments Promoting Good Governance Practices." Paper presented at the 11th International Anti-Corruption Conference, Seoul, South Korea, May 26–29. Workshop no. 5.6: Corruption and Donor Policies and Practices.

Richter, Rudolf, and Eirik Furubotn (2003). *Neue Institutionenökonomik: Eine Einführung und kritische Würdigung.* 3rd ed. Tübingen: Mohr Siebeck.

Rose-Ackerman, Susan (1998). "Corruption and Development." In Boris Pleskovi and Josef Stiglitz, eds., *Annual World Bank Conference on Development Economics 1997.* Washington, DC: World Bank.

Sacerdoti, Giorgio (1999). "Das OECD-Übereinkommen 1997 über die Bekämpfung der Bestechung ausländischer Amtsträger im internationalen Geschäftsverkehr." In Mark Pieth and Peter Eigen, eds., *Korruption im internationalen Geschäftsverkehr. Bestandsaufnahme, Bekämpfung, Prävention.* Neuwied: Luchterhand, pp. 212–227.

Schauenberg, Bernd (2000). "Korruption als Ordnungs- und als Organisationsproblem." In Bernhard Külp and Viktor Vanberg, eds., *Freiheit und wettbewerbliche Ordnung: Gedenkband zur Erinnerung an Walter Eucken.* Freiburg: Haufe.

Schmidt, Kurt (2003). "Korruption aus (vorwiegend) ökonomischer Sicht." In Verena von Nell, Gottfried Schwitzgebel, and Matthias Vollet, eds., *Korruption: Interdisziplinäre Zugänge zu einem kom-*

plexen Phänomen. Wiesbaden: Deutscher Universitäts-Verlag, pp. 87–97.

Schmidt, Kurt, and Christine Garschagen (1978). "Korruption." In *Handwörterbuch der Wirtschaftswissenschaft.* Band 4. Stuttgart: Fischer, Mohr, Vandenhoeck u. Ruprecht, pp. 565–573.

Shang, Ying (2002). "Curbing Corruption: A Comparative Analysis of Corruption Control in Singapore, Hong Kong, and Taiwan." Ph.D. diss., Harvard University(UMI Dissertation Service 3076914).

Sinaga, Kastorius (1994). "Beyond the Edge: An Assessment of Internal Limitations of Indonesian NGOs." In Rolf Hanisch and Rodger Wegner, eds., *Nichtregierungsorganisationen und Entwicklung: Auf dem Weg zu mehr Realismus.* Schriften des Deutschen Übersee-Instituts Hamburg, No. 28, pp. 99–118.

Singh, Kavaljit (2003). "Aid and Good Governance: A Discussion Paper for the Reality of Aid." 11th International Anti-Corruption Conference, Seoul, South Korea, May 26–29. Workshop no. 5.6: Corruption and Donor Policies and Practices.

Singh, Mritunjay (1999). "The Fight Against Business Corruption: Standards for Corporate Governance and Internal Control." In Mark Pieth and Peter Eigen, eds., *Korruption im internationalen Geschäftsverkehr: Bestandsaufnahme, Bekämpfung, Prävention.* Neuwied: Luchterhand, pp. 409–422.

Sklias, Pantelis G. (1999). *Non-Governmental Organisations and the International Political Economy, with Special Reference to the European Union's Development Policy.* Athens: Compupress.

Streissler, Erich (1981). "Zum Zusammenhang zwischen Korruption und Wirtschaftsverfassung: Korruption im Vergleich der Wirtschaftssysteme." In Christian Brünner, ed., *Korruption und Kontrolle.* Wien: Böhlau, pp. 299–328.

Stückelberger, Christoph (2003). "Continue Fighting Corruption. Experiences and Tasks of Churches and Development Agencies." Bread for All. Impulse No. 2/2003. Berne.

Tanzi, Vito, and Hamid Davoodi (1997). "Corruption, Public Investment, and Growth." Working Paper WP/97/139. Washington, DC: International Monetary Fund.

Tanzi, Vito, and Hamid Davoodi (1998). "Roads to Nowhere: How Corruption in Public Investment Hurts Growth." Economic Issues No. 12. Washington, DC: International Monetary Fund.

Tetzlaff, Rainer (1991). "Politische Eliten zwischen

Selbstbereicherung und Herrschaftslegitimation: Zur politischen Korruption in Entwicklungsländern." In *Korruption: Eine Herausforderung für Gesellschaft und Kirche*. Bad Boll: Evangelische Akademie. Protokolldienst 8/91, pp. 48–55.

Thornburgh, Dick (2004). Testimony before the US Senate Committee on Foreign Relations hearing, *Combating Multilateral Development Bank Corruption: U.S. Treasury Role and Internal Efforts*. July 21. http://www.foreign.senate.gov/hearings/2004/hrg040721a.html (27.03.2008).

Thornburgh, Dick, Ronald L. Gainer, and Cuyler H. Walker (2002). "Report Concerning the Debarment Processes of the World Bank." August 14 (Rev.). http://siteresources.worldbank.org/PROCUREMENT/Resources/thornburghreport.pdf (27.03.2008).

Transparency International (2002). "The Integrity Pact: The Concept, the Model, and the Present Applications: A Status Report." As of December 31, 2002. http://info.worldbank.org/etools/docs/library/238178/4.2.1%20i%5Fpact%5B1%5D.pdf (27.03.2008).

Transparency International (2003). "Corruption Fighters' Tool Kit." CD-ROM. Berlin: Transparency International.

Transparency International (2006). "Bribe Payers Index (BPI) 2006." Analysis Report. Berlin: Transparency International. http://www.transparency.org/policy_research/surveys_indices/bpi/bpi_2006 (15.12.2007).

United Nations Development Programme (1997). "Corruption and Good Governance." Discussion Paper 3. Management Development and Governance Division. Bureau for Policy and Programme Support. New York: UNDP, July.

Varese, Federico (1997). "The Transition to the Market and Corruption in Post-socialist Russia." *Political Studies* 45, no. 3, pp. 579–596.

Verhezen, Peter (2002). "Gifts and Alliances in Java." *Ethical Perspectives: Journal of the European Ethics Network* 9, no. 1, pp. 56–65.

Voslensky, Michael (1985). "Die korrupte Nomenklatura." In Christian Fleck and Helmut Kuzmics, eds., *Korruption: Zur Soziologie nicht immer abweichenden Verhaltens*. Königstein: Athenäum, pp. 159–174.

Wade, Robert (1985). "The Market for Public Office: Why the Indian State Is Not Better at Development." *World Development* 13, no. 4, pp. 467–497.

Watzlawick, Paul, Janet H. Beavin, and Don D. Jackson (1968). *Pragmatics of Human Communication: A Study of Interactional Patterns, Pathologies, and Paradoxes*. London: Faber and Faber.

Wegner, Rodger (1994). "Anspruch und Wirklichkeit in der nicht-staatlichen Entwicklungszusammenarbeit auf den Philippinen: Ein politologischer Diskussionsbeitrag." In Rolf Hanisch and Rodger Wegner, eds., *Nichtregierungsorganisationen und Entwicklung: Auf dem Weg zu mehr Realismus*. Schriften des Deutschen Übersee-Instituts Hamburg, No. 28, pp. 119–140.

Wei, Shang-Jin (1999). "Corruption in Economic Development: Beneficial Grease, Minor Annoyance, or Major Obstacle?" Harvard University and National Bureau of Economic Research. http://www.worldbank.org/wbi/governance/pdf/wei.pdf (27.03.2008).

Wei, Shang-Jin (2001). "Corruption in Economic Transition and Development: Grease or Sand?" UN Economic Commission for Europe Spring Seminar, Geneva, May 7. http://www.unece.org/ead/sem/sem2001/papers/Wei.pdf (27.03.2008). Revised version published in UNECE Economic Survey of Europe 2001, No. 2, pp. 101–112.

Wiehen, Michael H. (1999). "Auftragsvergabe." In Mark Pieth and Peter Eigen, eds., *Korruption im internationalen Geschäftsverkehr: Bestandsaufnahme, Bekämpfung, Prävention*. Neuwied: Luchterhand, pp. 492–518.

Wiehen, Michael H. (2001). "Transparency in Procurement." In Lara M. Gabriel and Rick Stapenhurst, with Mary Thomas, eds., *The Role of Bilateral Donors in Fighting Corruption*. Washington, DC: World Bank, pp. 85–93.

Wiehen, Michael H. (2003). "Avoiding/Containing Corruption in Privatization." GTZ-Handreichung. Manuscript.

Wolff, Jürgen H. (2001). "Köpfe oder Karzer? Das Schicksal von Gutachtern und Gutachten." *Epd-entwicklungspolitik*, nos. 11–12.

Wolff, Jürgen H. (2005). *Entwicklungshilfe: Ein hilfreiches Gewerbe? Versuch einer Bilanz*. Münster: Lit.

World Bank (1987). "Indonesia. Strategy for Economic Recovery." Report No. 6694-IND, May 5. Jakarta: World Bank.

World Bank (1997a). "Helping Countries Combat Corruption: The Role of the World Bank." PREM (Poverty Reduction and Economic Management). Washington, DC: World Bank.

http://www1.worldbank.org/publicsector/anticorrupt/corruptn/corrptn.pdf (04.01.2008).

World Bank (1997b). *The State in a Changing World: World Development Report 1997*. New York: Oxford University Press.

World Bank (2000). "Helping Countries Combat Corruption: Progress at the World Bank Since 1997." PREM (Poverty Reduction and Economic Management). Washington, DC: World Bank. http://info.worldbank.org/etools/docs/library/18414/helpingcountries.pdf (05.01.2008).

World Bank (2002a). "Reforming Public Institutions and Strengthening Governance: A World Bank Strategy." Implementation Update, Part 1: Overall Update. April. Washington, DC: World Bank. http://www1.worldbank.org/publicsector/StrategyUpdate1.pdf (05.01.2008).

World Bank (2002b). "Reforming Public Institutions and Strengthening Governance: A World Bank Strategy." Implementation Update, Part 2: Regional, DRG, and WBI Updates. April. Washington, DC: World Bank. http://www1.worldbank.org/publicsector/StrategyUpdate2.pdf (05.01.2008).

World Bank (2005). "Annual Report on Investigations and Sanctions of Staff Misconduct and Fraud and Corruption in Bank-Financed Projects." Fiscal Year 2004. Department of Institutional Integrity. Washington, DC: World Bank. http://siteresources.worldbank.org/INTDOII/Resources/INTFY04AnnualReport2005.pdf (06.01.2008).

World Bank (2006). "Guidelines Procurement Under IBRD Loans and IDA Credits." May 2004, revised October 1, 2006. http://siteresources.worldbank.org/INTPROCUREMENT/Resources/ProcGuid-10-06-ev1.doc (02.01.2008).

World Bank (2007a). "Annual Integrity Report: The World Bank Group, Fiscal Year 2005–2006." Washington, DC: World Bank. http://siteresources.worldbank.org/INTDOII/Resources/complete.pdf (05.01.2008).

World Bank (2007b). "Strengthening World Bank Group Engagement on Governance and Anticorruption." March 21. http://www.worldbank.org/html/extdr/comments/governancefeedback/gacpaper-03212007.pdf (05.01.2008).

World Bank (2008). "World Bank Listing of Ineligible Firms: Fraud and Corruption." http://web.worldbank.org/external/default/

main?theSitePK=84266&contentMDK=64069844&menuPK=116730&pagePK=64148989&piPK=64148984 (01.01.2008).

World Bank (undated). "Preventing Corruption in Bank Projects: Procurement Guidelines." http://wbln0018.worldbank.org/network/prem/premdoclib.nsf/6c8c7440a03ec7ae852566c60075b51c/6535268e0cd7de178525671300047 0c9?OpenDocument (05.01.2008).

World Bank Office, Jakarta, and the World Bank Department of Institutional Integrity (2002). "Fiduciary Review of the Second Sulawesi Urban Development Project." Overview Report. June. Jakarta: World Bank. http://lnweb18.worldbank.org/eap/eap.nsf/Attachments/SulawesiFROR0602/$File/SulawesiFROR0602.pdf (04.01.2008).

World Bank Resident Staff, Indonesia (1998). "Summary of RSI Staff Views Regarding the Problem of 'Leakage' from World Bank Project Budget. Internal Document." Published on the House of Commons website, http://www.parliament.the-stationery-office.co.uk/pa/cm200001/cmselect/cmintdev/39/39ap07.htm (05.01.2008).

Index

About the Book

ALTHOUGH CORRUPTION HAS ALWAYS BEEN A QUIETLY RECognized aspect of development aid programs, the taboo against openly discussing it is only now being widely overcome. Georg Cremer systematically addresses the subject, exploring the nature and impact of corruption, the conditions under which it is most likely to take hold, and the strategies that can enable aid organizations, both NGOS and those in the state sector, to limit the risk.

Georg Cremer is secretary general of Caritas Germany and associate professor of economics at the University of Freiburg. He has been extensively involved with aid programs in both Asia and eastern Europe.